Cycles of Resilience

Tiffany T. Ray

Self-Published by Tiffany Ray

Chicago, Illinois

Printed in the United States of America

Author Tiffany Ray

Cycles of Resilience

www.cyclesofresilience.com

cyclesofresilience@gmail.com

Book Design by Karl Ray of Karl Ray Photography

www.karlrayphotography.com

karlrayphotography@gmail.com

Book Cover Creative Director: Sheena Watkins

Book Cover Makeup Artist: Santanna Benford

signaturebyssheneal@gmail.com

Cover Dress provided by Bronzeville Boutique, Chicago, IL.

Book Consultant: Gary Norman Jr.

Luv2write@live.com

Editor 1: Sheena Watkins

Sheena.shardae@gmail.com

Editor 2: Mohamed Sherriff

-Cycles of Resilience-

DEDICATION

Psalm 82: 3-4 (NCV)

3 Defend the weak and the orphans; defend the rights of the poor and suffering.

4 Save the weak and helpless; free them from the power of the wicked.

Desiree Robinson. You are my "Why!"

TABLE OF CONTENTS

FOREWORD

By: Camille D. Robinson

The world is small.

So small that there is a possibility that we are connected in some small way to everyone in it. Either directly or indirectly. This statement of fact proved itself to be true when I discovered that one of my best friends from church who I had grown up with and had known for over 20 years was in fact my cousin. Even more amazing was that she was not the only one.

Tiffany is my cousin. By blood? By marriage? I don't know. Who is connected to who that's connected to us that connects us to each other? I couldn't tell you. What I can tell you is that family, no matter how it is constructed, is to stick together.

That's what I was taught, even though I may not always have witnessed it first-hand.

Tiffany is the one I didn't see much, but I knew existed. In fact, I was closer with her eldest sister, who I spoke to often, and inquired about her health and her children on a regular basis. Tiffany was the one who always talked to me through Facebook. Her comments were limited but they always stuck out to me because she always called me "Cousin" and I was always trying to figure out who she was and how we were connected.

I never remembered her more than that random day I got this phone call out of the blue. I was stunned because everyone knows I'm not a phone person. I'd rather receive a text than to actually pick up the phone and talk to someone. I can't tell you where I was or what I was doing, but I can tell you I remember pieces of this day like it was yesterday. I saw her name pop up on the caller ID and I remember thinking, "Why is she calling me? We don't talk like that!" I was tempted to ignore it and send the call to voicemail but my spirit urged me to answer. Why? *Because we don't talk like that.* Her voice sounded so weak and exhausted like she had been up all night.

"Hey Cousin", she managed to whisper. I knew something was wrong. I sensed it. So, I indulged. I made room for her and I listened to her give me her heart. Piece by shattered piece. I could not believe the things she was telling me and I was stunned to stillness until my mouth found the words.

"Tiffany? Get...out."

I heard the anguish and fear in her voice. The desire to want to move but not knowing where to go or even how to make the first step. I remember telling her that I don't care what she had to do, but she had to leave. She had to save her own life. She couldn't wait on anyone else to do it for her. I don't think I even fully understood what was happening or what she was running from. All I knew was that she was in danger and she had to go. Now. She was not guaranteed the opportunity to leave again. The more I talked to her, the more I felt my spirit urging hers. I saw myself running through a wooded area. Nothing around me but barren trees, twigs, leaves, and dead grass. It was overcast. No sunshine. No promise. Not knowing where I was going or where I would end up. Just running. I stayed on the phone with

Tiffany. Urging her. Willing her. Encouraging her. I needed her to run with me. The more we talked, the more I prayed, and the more she started to formulate a plan. She thought of people she could call. She thought of places she could go. Once she seemed like her head was a little clearer, I began to hear the hope in her voice and I prayed with all my might that the ones she intended to seek for help would not let her down. I made her promise me that once she was safe, that she would call me. For the first time on a very rare occasion, I was in anticipation for a phone call. When my phone finally rang, it was her telling me that she was on her way home and that she would contact me when she arrived safely.

Time passed and it took a minute, but Tiffany worked to reconnect and reconcile. With her family, with her church, and with her children. During that time, I may not have seen her or talked to her often, but I became overprotective of her. I commented on almost every post, wanted to know where she was, who she was with, and how long before she returned. At times, she jokingly called me "Mama". I didn't care. She was finally free. There was no way I would watch her slip back into the darkness again. Most times, we'd disagree, but I knew she appreciated me looking out for her from afar. She didn't take the path that most would have. She may not have done all the right things or made the best choices, but whatever she had gone through made her into a survivor. She was determined and she would not quit. With every success, with every positive outcome, I began to see the cloud removed from her. She began to glow from the inside out. What she went through beat her up, but it didn't kill her. I look at this beautiful warrior now, and I thank God for her every time I see her face. Because I know where she's been, but I also see how far she's come and I'm excited about where she's headed.

She is a child of God, a wife, a mother, a daughter, a sister, a friend, an advocate, a SURVIVOR. One thing she is not...is a victim. And now it is time to tell her story as only she can because, in this small world where we are all connected, someone is surely listening. I pray you find strength in every word.

PREFACE

A little girl made a woman overnight by men who had no respect for her innocence. They used her for their sick and wicked pleasures which planted a seed of self-hatred within her that would eventually blossom with devastating consequences. She would be wounded by men devoid of well intent and love and that was okay with her. She never knew what real love looked like so the deceitful wolf hidden underneath the trustworthy sheep's clothing always won. But that too would pass, or so she thought. Just when she thought the days of being taken advantage of were behind her, she soon learned that the worst was yet to come. At last, feeling the freedom of bliss only to be fooled by an ingenious plot and again hoodwinked. She was on a quest to search her soul.

-Cycles of Resilience-

ACKNOWLEDGEMENTS

God, Thank you for my life.

Thank you to My Crew for loving me despite of…

My husband, Karl Ray, thank you for your unconditional love and support.

My children, Mariah, Tyrone and Taylor, thank you for allowing me to regain your love and trust. Thank you for accepting me.

To my Queens that have inspired and uplifted me to be a better woman, I love you forever ladies. Thank you!

J. Adrienne, Santanna Benford, Roncita Johnson, Regina Jones, Serita Love, Tavara Morris, Tally Ray, Camille Robinson, Treva Salaam, Deetria Scott, Erica Walton, Sheena Watkins and Jeri Wright.

PROLOGUE

When you are young and broken… When your life is without

loved ones… When your mind is without discernment… You

make the same mistakes over and over and over… Until… the

Grace of God spares you.

Ch. 1

Trans-Generational Nightmare

The year, 1983. Life birthed through mother's womb sculpting a pale skinned, freckled face baby girl with fire red hair. Did mother kiss me, hold me or love on me? If not, signs of maternal disconnection were set forth from conception.

Was father awaiting my arrival? Did he caress my hand and promise me his best? Did he hand me over to the nurses out of shame because of the way I looked? Or was he even there? Many unanswered questions leave inquisitive entries into worlds placement for the future.

Place; middle-class neighborhood on the southside of Chicago called Gresham. There were many people with multiple personalities and chaos at every turn in my home. My grandparents birthed seven children and raised an additional six grandchildren. Two of my grandparents' children had passed away, and the other five had their own set of obstacles to overcome. There were two uncles; one with brain damage my grandparents nursed back to health from near death, and the other uncle who was an alcoholic and woman beater. My two aunts; one with a gambling issue and the other who was too bougie for her own good. And my mom, who was an alcoholic and drug addict. There were also three male cousins who were the sons of my uncle who had brain damage. I looked up to all three of them as if they were my blood brothers. However, all three were gang affiliated, drug dealers and ran the streets.

With so many people raised in the home, we never received that one on one love we needed to grow and develop into mature young adults. We found ourselves clashing quite often and that caused tension to arise within the home. Every single person was competing for the love and affection of my grandparents who tried very hard, the best they knew, to disperse it evenly and effectively.

Sex was everywhere, yet no one relinquished guidance of the do's and don'ts in regard to the spectrum of sexual intercourse. I remember my grandmother saying to me, "You can always come to talk to me about anything". But, when it was time to talk about the act of sex the response was, "I don't want to talk about that. It's wrong and you better not be doing it." She made it seem like it was such a terrible thing. But in reality, if it was explained to me at the proper age and in the proper manner I would have possibly learned what to do and what not to do. Not knowing played a major part in the cycle my life took in reference to sexual behavior. We all need that one person whom we can truly talk to about any and everything without judgement or fear.

My mother spent more time in rehab centers than she spent with family because of her drug addiction. I didn't realize it then but her absence made each of us, her children, grow up looking at life through harsh-reality colored glasses with no protection from life's blinding dire consequences.

Each of my mother's children had their own way of coping with her absence. Not saying either was the right or wrong way. My eldest sister; Ms. Uptight, the world belongs to me kind of girl who was spoiled rotten. The rod was certainly spared for her. My middle sister; Ms. Manipulative, turned into one of the biggest bullies in the family. And me; Ms. Misunderstood, outspoken and only desired love from my family. Without our mother there to mold us, we were forced to figure out life alone at a very early age.

We were raised as Christians attending church every Sunday. My grandparents instilled morals and values in a simplistic manner which was to the best of their ability. I personally enjoyed church and the fulfillment of my spirit. I started singing in the children's choir at the age of five and loved attending Sunday school and bible study, all of which made me extremely happy. As the years progressed, I found myself being one of the top youth leaders of the church. I sat on many ministries as the youth coordinator, the only teen during that time to take seat on several adult ministries. Around the age of fifteen, I was consecrated as a Junior Deacon. This was a huge accomplishment seeing that it was a very spiritual time in my life. Six days a week I would volunteer at the college placement office of the church. Being involved in the teenage choir was an awesome experience. The friendships that were made I will never forget. The lessons I learned from my mentors I'll forever cherish. They were phenomenal individuals and added value to my life. I learned a lot through their experiences of life and Christ. There came a time when I began to feel the pressure of not being able to enjoy my spiritual moments in the church. Once I was home, I was forced into being someone I wasn't. And on top of that, grandmother would fuss and punish me for spending majority of my free time at the church house. Church had been my escape from home until I could no longer retreat and was trapped in a spin cycle of life. It was my safe haven.

A few of my fondest memories as a little girl was hanging out with all my aunts and female cousins. The best times were taking trips to go shopping with them and my grandmother. Sitting at my grandfather's bedside while he watched football games were timeless and priceless memories I wish I could get back. In the morning, I enjoyed being next to him at the kitchen table when he would read the Chicago Sun-Times newspaper with his oatmeal and coffee. Spending quality time with my grandfather was very instrumental to my growth process as I matured with trying to understand men. When he passed away there lived an emptiness and void in my heart. He didn't speak much, he was a very quiet man. His actions displayed love, care and a peace that I was fortunate enough to witness. He never let anything negative get to him and if so, he never displayed it to his family or the public eye.

I also enjoyed playing hide and seek with my sisters and a male cousin or playing outside in the backyard on the swing set. I loved dressing up in my oldest sister's clothing especially when she was not home. I would pretend to be her and emulate her jumping rope and playing hop scotch. I loved when my grandmother would dress my sister's and I like little dolls. There were the beautiful dresses which had bows and the ribbons in our hair to match as we prepared ourselves for whatever event we were attending.

I had many good times as a child, but the bad definitely outweighed the good. My life would never be the same. I felt as if I was targeted as things unfortunately started to turn for the worst. Due to my mother and father's actions or lack thereof, my life would never reach the expectations I envisioned in my mind. I was lost in dreamland trying to recall happiness.

Mother and Father, where were you? I wanted my adolescent life to look like one of my best friends at the time. Both parents in the home, loving and kind, full of energy and joy. I wished I had her life. Thanks for not parenting, parents.

"Challenges make you discover things about yourself that you never really knew."

-Cicely Tyson-

-Cycles of Resilience-

Ch. 2

When 1+1=Denial

Mother's drug addiction was selfish and she only thought of her next score. My sister's and I were in pain yet yearning mother's love. Functionality was scarce; shame and hurt followed the realization that she is still our mother. Saying those words out loud hurt like twenty lashes across a bare back. To witness how she sacrificed everything and everyone for her selfish ways and substance abuse was devastating. At such a young age, I really did not understand what was happening. Mom was living in and out of the home. Whenever she felt like leaving us, she up and left returning when she felt it was time to be a mom. I just knew I wanted my mother and I wanted to love her no matter what anyone else had to say about her. And the family had plenty negative opinions about mother. *She's mine, not yours, so back off.*

Then there came story time with grandmother, which was always a treat until she got to the part about how her daughter, my mother, left me at church never to return. I was only a few weeks into life. I inherited desolate, cold and lonely traits. *Mind roaming!* Why would she abandon me? Did someone make her give me away? Why didn't she love me? Was father secretly a part of the church? *Hmm…* Did a person exude diabolical traumatizing actions upon her? Did those actions push her into one bad relationship after another with men that she felt she so desperately needed?

Men who would slap, spit and beat her. Drugs were granted as long as those men were sexually satisfied. I was around seven years old when I witnessed a man with a bat, position himself to hit a homerun with my mother's face. LL Cool J's, "Mama Said Knock You Out" was blasting from the man's car radio. Trembling, I screamed, "Please don't hit my mommy, please!" He let her live only to revisit my mom's bad habits again later. She would disappear from home for days at a time knowing that there were consequences for her actions like beatings, rape, starvation and isolation.

Disoriented, I would blindly search for my mother's love while she vanished from her emotional state of being. Mom would seek placebo love which would allow men to take control over her mind. They would say, "I'll give you my money, just stay with me. I won't hit you again. I won't rape you. I won't harm you. I can't live without you baby. I love you so much." Mother fell for it every time and the abuse continued. The bottom line was, through it all, they never wanted her to leave them.

Having an absentee father was devastating and disappointing as a young girl. Who was I to become? What would people think of me? He didn't tell me it only matters what you think of yourself. Who was going to love me? I needed my father to love me. Feeling like a wayward child, walking alone with no direction and undaunted courage. I had no proper structure of love from those I needed most.

12

Emotional, mental and spiritual scars took their toll on me. I needed daddy to hug me in the morning hours and tuck me in at night fall. His role was to show me how to love a man properly. I longed to hear those three magical words, "Daddy loves you." Every daddy loves, cherishes and shows off his little girl. How could he leave me? I'm suffering Daddy. I need you.

With no instruction from mother or father, how do I trust men? How do I trust myself with men? What do I look for in a man? With no role model beside men who abused my mother, I was destined to find out the hard way that men wore all types of masks to hide their deficiencies.

"When someone shows you who they are, believe them the first time."

-Maya Angelou-

Ch. 3

A Pawn in Mama's Hand

I have suffered a great deal of pain centered on mother and father actions or lack thereof. Mother would often take me with her to retrieve her narcotics. There were moments she would leave me to be cared for by her drug dealers and fellow users. The psychological and emotional damage I endured or felt was mother's fault beginning in my adolescent years. I have always wondered if my mom genuinely cared enough for me not to let things take place like me being molested in my early years. The mental anguish it caused was that of not trusting anyone in my life. I hate that she was never there to protect me. Mom, why did you leave me to be eaten and swallowed by the world's most demonic people?

Two of those individuals were longtime friends of the family. They grew up with my aunts and uncles only a few houses from my grandparent's home where I was raised. My mother would often sneak me out of the house when my grandparents would leave and go to the grocery store or run errands. We would walk only a few houses down to get her drugs. I'm not sure if she had all the money needed to score but I do know when my mom would go into the next room so I would not see her getting high. I in exchange, was being molested by her friends. I could not believe she did not hear my screams for help. Calling out to her, "Mommy, please help me. They are hurting me." They were performing acts on me as if I were a grown woman. They started off being nice and sweet "uncles" offering me food and beverages. But that all ended, as they moved in slowly toward me asking me to give them a hug. As I would hug them, believing they were like family and trusting them; they began to caress my genitalia slowly with their fingers covering my mouth In hopes that no one could hear my screams for help. While kissing me in the mouth with their tongue after I had been told to keep quiet, I would be asked, "How does it feel?" It felt weird and I knew what they were doing to me was wrong. They rapidly removed

16

my clothing before my mother came out of the next room. As my clothing dropped to the floor I was told to open my mouth where it would be penetrated with one of their shafts. The other man would continue to rub my genitalia with his tactile members. I was instructed to lie on the cold cemented floor and spread my legs. I squeezed my legs tightly together putting up a battle not to be forced into the act of sexual behavior. The strength of both men overpowered and outweighed my infinitesimal structure. They forced themselves upon me and raped me. Weeping for the help of my mother went unanswered as I was being defiled. She never responded to me and never came to my rescue. Once they finished raping me, I was left on the floor tucked into a fetal shell and bleeding from the lower half of my body. Once my plundering violators saw the blood, they grabbed tissue and fastened it into my vaginal area. With a knife held to my throat I was told by my rapists that if I told anyone they would murder me and my entire family. I nodded my head in acknowledgment of understanding the severity of speaking a word of this to anyone, ever. An hour later or so later, my mother resurfaced not in the same state of being as she went into the next room. She was extremely high and unaware of the situation at hand. Mother walked me home as if nothing ever happened. I ran into my room climbed into my bed and cried myself to sleep. I never spoke a word of this to anyone, ashamed and afraid. I pretended as if it never came to pass knowing the consequences of what my molesters would do to my entire family who said they would murder them. I was raped on a reoccurring basis for the next five years of my life.

At thirteen years old, I felt as though I had gained enough courage to finally speak up and tell one of my older male cousins that I trusted. As I formulated the words to him that I had been raped over the years and asked for his help, he immediately denied that it happened to me. He advised me not say anything to the family about it because It would cause contusion and disaster, otherwise he would harm me. I could not comprehend why he did not take me at my word. How could he, a male figure in my life, my own flesh and blood not believe me? I was in a state of shock and felt alone even more than I had previously.   Sometime later in my adult years, he confessed to me that he too had been raped by a male member of our family and never told anyone. He was also holding on to his own past anguish, guilt, hurt, pain and confusion. I believed him and wanted to help him get the help he needed. But what I was uncertain of was how he would negate the fact that I was also raped, as if that was the normal actions of our family life.

I also discovered years later into my adulthood that my cousin was the bag-man that supplied the same men that were molesting me with the drugs they were supplying to my mother. That within itself enlightened my understanding that my cousin may have known I was molested all those years and never came to my rescue. He was solely focused on making money and not concerned with the desire of saving my life. I no longer have a relationship with my cousin who I simply adored at one point in life and treated as if he were my brother and my best friend.

There was something that dismantled my concept of family life, which also caused a uniquely interesting, disturbing and disgusting thought process in my later years in life. It was the fact that my molesters could potentially be my biological father and uncle. Roughly around three years ago, my great aunt on my mother's side of the family, who took a major role into molding me spirituality passed away. She was my spiritual foundation, instructor and guided me through the tender touch of God's hand. She made sure I continued to keep focus on The Creator no matter what the storm. I miss you dearly Auntie...

The day of her funeral an old childhood friend approached me and asked if she could speak with me. I asked her to give me a few moments as I was preparing our guests to eat at the funeral repast, which was held at my grandmother's home. Some time had passed and I walked a few houses down to this female friend's apartment. She seemed to have been dismayed, offended or stunned of whatever it was she needed to disclose with me. She invited me into her apartment and requested I take a seat. She informed me that her father could also be my father. So many humiliating thoughts arose in my mind and I began to get angry with the thoughts of my childhood molestation memories. I asked how did she come to the know-how of this news. She explained to me that my middle sister was home washing dishes in her kitchen and our mother was also there keeping an eye on her grandchildren. My mother walked into the kitchen where my sister was standing at the sink and says to her, "Your friend's father is your baby sister's birth father" and immediately returned to tending to her grandchildren. My friend then goes on to say my sister called her and told her the newly found information. My sister immediately jumped in her car and headed over to our friend's home. What I could not understand was the thought of my sister not being able to pick up her telephone to simply have a conversation with me about this. I'm not sure where the disconnection between my sister and I began, but a phone call could have been the beginning stage of our healing process together.

I requested that my friend returned with me to my grandmother's home where most of my late aunts' friends were leaving and all that was left at the home was immediate family. Everyone was in the living and dining rooms talking amongst themselves. I demanded the attention of my family and informed them of the details I received from my friend in regards to my biological father. As she was standing with me in the center of both rooms, I asked my family if she and I resembled one another. My family halted their conversations and agreed that she and I looked just alike. They asked, "Why are you asking Tiffany?" I replied, "She informed me that my mother confirmed that her dad was also my biological father." Some of my family members were not shocked at all. One of my uncles and a few cousins said they already knew that he was my father. I asked them why they did not tell me after all of my searching efforts. My family said that it was not for them to tell me and it was my mother's responsibility to communicate that with me. My friend asked if I wanted to have a DNA test taken to see if we were indeed sisters. I told her I wasn't sure if I was ready for that. That meant I would have to take a DNA test with my friend, being as though, both her father and uncle who had passed away prior to being informed, could possibly be my paternal father and uncle. That was something I was not ready to face. They both experienced tragic deaths from drug overdoses to my knowledge, in the same basement apartment they molested me in three houses from my grandparent's home where I was brought up. How ironic was that?

Searching for my father has not been a walk in the park. I have asked my mom well over a couple hundred times to be honest and tell me who my father was. Either she would refuse to disclose it or say It could have been multiple men or an argument would begin, perhaps even a physical altercation would arise. She had an overwhelming anger toward me for wanting to know the truth. At times, I wondered if she did not know who he was. I would have felt a little better if that was her truth and she would have been open and honest enough to tell me. Whatever had taken place in her life previously and when I was born was not in the control of my hands. If someone did something to her like what was done to me I would have been able to identify with her. I expressed the need for her to be honest with me and confront the issue head on. That conversation has never brought us any closure.

I have taken several DNA tests where the men have not been my father; zero percent probability in all six cases. In pursuing my paternal father's whereabouts, I discovered my mother's love for tall, light skinned, freckled faced, red head men. Every single man I have tested with or heard about that could potentially be my true father had the same characteristics. A preacher man, a mercantile exchange broker, both of my molesters, a family friend and so many more all had the traits of her unique taste. Each time I would go to her and inform her I had taken the test she'd be infuriated or not even bother entertaining the conversation. She would either walk away from me or wave it off. She would curse me out saying things like, "You're a bitch and I hate you. I should not have ever had you. You are a waste of sperm. I should have killed you a long time ago. I should have had an abortion with you. I should have flushed you down the toilet. You deserve nothing in the world and every time I get a chance, I'm going to beat your ass and make your life miserable." However, these exact words have been expressed to me by her from the time I can remember as a young child. I was accustomed to the way she spoke hatred into my very existence. Mother gave me no other choice but to move on without her in my life and have minimum contact with her. When we would see one another, we could not spend more than five minutes in the same space, otherwise she wanted to play the role of the mother and that is something she had never been to me.

Around the age of five or six, I wrote my first suicide letter to my grandparents. The content of the letter was to inform my family that I could no longer stay in their family. I told them I felt like everyone hated me and I wished God would take me away from them. I was tired of getting beat for things such as leaving the water running in the bathroom sink while brushing my teeth or not eating all of my dinner. I would be beaten because my sisters would always blame me for the irresponsible things they would do themselves. Being the baby sister wasn't all that it was cracked up to be. I assumed that the youngest child received special treatment and considered the favorite child but that was not the case for me. A child being spanked in our household in the 80's & 90's was normal behavior but it was too much for me to handle. By the time I turned eight years old, the beatings became worse. After the first time I was molested I wanted to kill myself. I could not bear living with the thoughts of what happened to me. I addressed my second suicide letter to my grandmother and included with that was my last will and testament. At that time, I was hurt and confused because I was a little girl who was raped and had no one to turn to. I figured it wouldn't matter to anyone if I was dead. I thought out very carefully how I was going to kill myself. One of the two attic bedrooms I shared with my sister closest in age to me was the place I would start the process of dying. I planned on taking some of my grandmother's medication from her bedroom. Once everyone in the house was sleeping, I thought I could steal the pills from her and not get caught.

As I was writing my final letter, my sister caught me and began reading it. She stole the letter from my hands, ran downstairs and into my grandmother's bedroom. I chased behind her and by the time I reached grandmother's room she was already reading the short letter describing how much I hated all my family and wanted to take my life.

There was a household full of family and I knew I would be crucified by them all for what I wanted to do to myself. Grandmother called for grandfather, my mother, cousins, sisters, aunts and uncles to come into her room. Grandmother told me to have a seat on her bedroom floor. She instructed one of my sisters to get her infamous belt that she beat all the

27

children of the family with from her dresser drawer. As my sister was searching for the belt, my grandmother read the letter aloud for everyone to hear. I felt humiliated and wanted to die right before their eyes. My grandmother began calling me stupid and dumb. She told me if I wanted to die she should kill me in front of all of them. She taunted me with vile persuasions of hateful words as she and everyone cursed me out. I began banging my head against the dresser extremely hard trying to cause damage to myself. I was called every name in the book beside my own name. I was told I was ignorant and I should be sent to the "crazy house." She told me I needed psychiatric treatment and she was going to call the police to come get me from her home and have me committed. While everyone was laughing and pointing fingers at me, I closed my eyes and envisioned that I was already dead. I heard my name being called and did not respond. My grandmother said "Bitch get up, I know you hear me!" I opened my eyes while standing and noticed she had her belt in hand and I knew she was going to beat me.

This infamous belt of hers had a name and was made of leather, cut into nine strips like a whip. I felt like I was trapped in slavery being beaten by master himself. Grandmother's belt was called "The Cat" which was short for the "cat of nine tails." After my beating, grandmother told me to run myself a hot bath where I would have to submerge in the bathtub with open cuts and bleeding from my legs. I was forced to sit in the tub of scolding hot water and the more resistant I was to getting in the water, the more threats of bodily harm were directed toward me.

After my punishment of beating and bathing, I retreated to my bedroom and gazed out of the window. I gently opened the window and contemplated jumping out of it landing on the ground, dead. I was ready to jump but I heard a voice say, "No my child, I have better plans for your life." I didn't realize at the time it was my Heavenly Father talking to me as if He were standing right next to me. He gave me words of encouragement to stick it out and suicide was not the way my life would be ending. The Creator has been my saving grace from the time I was a child. I walked over to my bed kneeling down and prayed to God that He help my family learn to love and trust me.

"Your silence will not protect you."

-Audre Lorde-

-Cycles of Resilience-

Ch. 4

When I Thought I knew It All?

The admission of comparison within romantic affairs as my mother displayed came my lack of confidence with abstaining from the temptations of a beautifully dark clouded sphere of men in my teenage years, for that is all I knew by example. As I launched into dating, I encountered men who would pursue the depersonalization of me. They were drawn to me and I to them. I endowed interest in a man ten years my senior, a local drug dealer and I at the time was sixteen years old. Oh, how his fast lingo and fast life thrilled me in every sexual way. He dazzled me with the finest fashion designs and foot wear to rival with. He escorted me to five-star restaurants where he catered to me as if I were his 1st place prize, a princess to be reckoned with. We shared long lasting conversations about living the "good life" and washing the painful memories of everyone in our lives away. But as quickly

32

as his expensive taste and exotic mannerisms excited me, he began portraying many things that were already displayed from my childhood. I knew better than moving forward with this relationship but I could not turn him down for I was swiftly tangled in his web. For example, he instituted the use of profane language toward me for not responding to his telephone calls when we were not in the presence of one another. That was the same time he accused me of cheating on him. I previously opened up to him about what I experienced as a child and I believe that it did not help the situation with him being able to trust me. He took my deepest, darkest, most humiliating secrets and used them against me. He would say things to me while arguing, "You were born a whore so why should I believe anything you have to say." The relationship quickly became physically abusive and I stayed as long as I could simply because he treated me to all the finer things in life and I just knew I loved him. He eventually left me and found another young girl that he could use and when finished with her, throw away with the trash. My time was up as I was old news with a suitcase full of childhood issues. Soon after, there was a long line of men I sought after that was similar to the previous one I dated. Take a number, stand in line and wait your turn. I'll get to you all soon. That was my attitude and understanding at the time, use a man just like men have used you.

The pleasures of worldly vices had me in a downward spiraling trance. I could not rid myself of the fascinating temptations of raunchy fellows. A profoundly speaking man with an educational orientation was captivating and hypnotizing. Warped in his essence, I never took the time to familiarize myself with knowing him for who he really was. I would fall in love fairly quickly with him. Nothing else in the world mattered, only him. Whatever he wanted and whatever he said I would oblige. If he needed me to wait on him hand and foot I had no problems with that. Submitting to him without understanding the definition of submission. I would literally bow to him. I laid down with him and gave him my body whenever he desired. I did all those things without knowing what I was entering into. As time went on, I found myself referring back to my mother as I began to be beaten by the man I thought I loved. Day after day, night after night, he would abuse me. I had become numb to the beatings. I found myself desiring more of it. It pained me yet at the same time excited me for I thought this was true love. This is what I was taught by the examples and actions shown by my mother and male cousins. I assumed this was totally natural and normal behavior. After months of the same routine, he eventually became bored with me and commenced upon his search for other women. He was angrily irritated with me for no longer desiring the beatings or wanting to be involved in sexual intercourse whenever he wanted. But to keep him happy and all to myself, I gave into his demands and told him he could have me whenever he wanted. Even if I wasn't in the mood or had a busted face with bruises covering my body, I gave him the best of me. I told him that he could have me anytime of the day or night just as long as he did not leave me. He soon ended his search for other women and I was pleased. Early one morning while I was sound asleep, I awakened to him on top of me taking care of his physical pleasures. I refused his advances and said, "No I did not want to have sex with you." He began slapping and punching me in the face while on top of me until I passed out. As I awakened, I felt pain in the lower half of my body and realized he raped me. My body was screaming for help and out of my mouth I began screaming, "Get off of me, I don't want this, somebody help me!" And that pissed him off terribly. The louder I shouted the more he would force his penis into me as if it was turning him on. The moment I was able to escape from him is the moment I ran straight into the arms of another man. But this time, this man was a married man.

Dealing with married men was one of my conquests I had to fulfill. The chase excited my being. I wanted to see how it felt to have sex with them knowing I may have been caught by their wives. I was excited to sneak around their homes searching for places to hide a remembrance of me for their wives to find. I did that because I wanted that man to know how his wife would feel if she caught him cheating. I wondered if he cared that he was jeopardizing all he had worked for to provide a life for his family. In a way, I wanted him to feel how I felt once he was done invading my body. I wanted him to feel ashamed for what he had done with me. I wanted him to know that everything that's done in the dark would definitely come to light. I wanted him to get cursed out and put out of the home he shared with his wife. I wanted him to feel the pain I was feeling when laying with him giving him all of me. I wanted to remind him that cheating on his wife had major consequences and I wanted to know if he would risk his life for mine.

A lot of married men that I had slept with always promised they would leave their wives for me. I needed to see if they really meant it but inside my mind I knew that they would never leave their mate for a side chick who could only offer him an orgasm. After many tries to identify with men would leave their wives for me, I came up with zero men. None of them wanted to deal with the headaches of a nagging side chick who only wanted money and materialistic goods from him. He only wanted one thing and when he got that from me he went on about his business. He no longer answered my restricted calls or responded to any of my attempts to reach him even if I showed up at his job causing a scene. Not responding to me set a fire under my ass to look for him in all his known hangout spots. If ever I would see him I didn't know what I was going to do. I wasn't sure if I was going to slap him in the face or curse him out for the dog he was. I contemplated begging him to take me back because I was lonely and miserable. I needed him and he made it very obvious that he wanted no parts of me. I felt ashamed and thrown away to the trash. My body would go through withdrawals and I'd be sick for days, even weeks at a time because I needed him. The phone calls stopped coming in. The dates were over and I was left to deal with the guilt and shame for what I had done. I purposely tried to tear apart a family who knew nothing of me and I didn't care. I desired what I wanted and was not in the business of compromising for anyone. I was miserable and wanted the wives to feel my misery for not satisfying their husband to a point where he sought to find a damsel in distress to cure his sexual appetite. After all my attempts to get a married man to leave his wife, I took a long break from sex because it had sent me through some of the worst mental battles I would experience. But once I was back in the swing of things, I figured I'd try my luck on a man younger than myself.

I went without pursuing sex for roughly a year. When the interest sparked to feel someone inside me I needed to make sure I still knew how to rock the boat. I felt the only way to prepare myself for a real man was to find a younger man that I could test the waters with. The thrills of a younger man had me in a head space like Stella when she got her groove back. I needed to make sure kitty could still purr. A younger man had more stamina than any man I had come across before him. He taught me many new positions that I eventually used on the next subject matter. Once I was almost finished with him, I had to play mind games because he was warped in my sexual trance and I had to find a way to let him down gently. But on the course of our intimate adventures, he had fallen in love with me. How in the world would I be able to get rid of him now? I realized the only thing I had to do to rid myself of him was to use the same psychology that was once upon a time used to trick me. I would tell him he was acting like a little boy and that he was not a real man and that he didn't know what to do with all this woman and that he couldn't get a woman like me in his wildest dreams. I also told him that he was terrible in bed and I faked every single orgasm. Those words crushed his heart because he thought he had a chance to be with me on a long-term basis. I wasn't honest with him and I could have told him what I wanted from him in the beginning. But again, I was in it for the thrill of it and now it was time for me to move on.

"The true worth of a race must be measured by the character of its womanhood."

-Mary McLeod Bethune-

-Cycles of Resilience-

Ch. 5

Candidate for Disaster

As I progressed into early adulthood and moved out of Chicago at the age of seventeen, I relocated to Arkansas to finish out my senior year of high school. And to watch over my mother who had followed her recently new boyfriend there. While living in Arkansas, I became pregnant with my first child at the age of eighteen. That infuriated my mother and she had no problem with me dropping out of high school my senior year. She was ashamed of me. She advised me I would be better off dropping out of school and getting a job because she was not going to help raise my child. My mother said I was doing the right thing by making my unborn child my number one priority. I attended school until one month before my graduation. I was told by my school's administration that I had enough credits to participate in the graduation ceremony. I was only one half of a credit short from receiving my high school diploma. I was devastated and embarrassed walking across the stage with all of my classmates to receive an empty diploma packet. I was made by my mother to pose for the cameras with having to leave the diploma packet closed. A few of my classmates requested to see my diploma. Tears swelled in my eyes and I ran to the closest exit as quickly as I could. I was so embarrassed and needed to escape from the lies. I could not believe I let my drug addicted mother convince me to become a drop out of school. I knew I had all the potential in the world to become anything I wanted. The month before graduation, when I was forced to quit school and find a job, my mother had me watch her home while drug dealers entered with pounds of uncut cocaine. I had never seen so many bricks of drugs in my life. Is this what my life was meant to be? The watchman for mother's drug operation...

I had been too embarrassed to go back to school to get my GED; even though I wanted to, I could never force myself to go. Mother sabotaged my life and I did not recognize it at the time. Nine months had passed and a beautiful baby girl was born. The same baby girl my mother tried to kill while she was in my womb. Mother was intoxicated with drugs and upset that I would not come out of my room to watch the house while she stepped away to party with her drug addicted neighbors one warm southern evening. I was roughly eight months pregnant when she came into my room and dragged me out of my bed by my hair. She began kicking me around the floor and told me if I could not do as I was told to get out of her house. I stood to my feet and told mother I did not need anything from her. I walked to my bedroom and started packing an overnight bag because I was going to stay at one of my girlfriend's home. Mother rushed me from behind and told me I could not take anything from her house. I told her that was fine by me and walked toward the front door. As I opened the door mother told me to face her and as I did, she raised her foot and kicked me in my stomach. Mother was yelling antics like, "I hate you and your child and I am going to kill you both." I remember lying on the ground on my backside as she stood over me and told me

44

to never come back. Our neighbors overheard the confusion and came to my rescue. They called an ambulance and I was taken to the local hospital to be treated and checked on the health of my unborn child. After leaving the hospital, I had no place else to go so I returned home and begged my mother to let me stay with her until I found my own apartment.

By the time my daughter was three months old, I secured my own place of residence. I thank God I had previously applied for governmental housing assistance. I called the office of housing authority and requested they put a rush on my housing application for I was about to become homeless with my baby. One week before my deadline to get out of my mother's home was a letter addressed to me, stating I had been approved for housing. I was a high school drop out with a newborn child and working two full time jobs. Life didn't seem so bad but it would have been much better with a high school diploma and a college degree. I birthed my first beautiful daughter and two years later my handsome baby boy.

I was to a point of wanting to relocate to my native town of Chicago. The man I was dating at the time was very abusive and I wanted to kill him. I could not take too much more of the physical violence and abandoned him. I telephoned my grandmother to inform her I would be moving back home and she welcomed me to live with her.

As time moved forward, I birthed my third child, another beautiful baby girl. Working in downtown Chicago raising my children and living my life the way I saw fit. Living in the home with my grandparents was also my aunt, who was not always the most pleasant person to encounter. My aunt had a way of infecting the lives of others around her in such a negative way. She reminds me of the saying, "misery loves company." She was evil on one hand and on the other she portrayed herself to be a sweet lady. She would smile in your face and attack your character behind your back. I bared witness to this behavior on numerous occasions amongst the members of the family. She carried herself in a manner of thinking she was better than everyone else although she too had an addiction. Her addiction was gambling at the casino. She would spend her last dime at the casino to fulfill her high. She is the negative matriarch of the family and had a way of poisoning the minds and spirits of those nearest to her without them fully understanding that they were being mentally bullied for her own personal gain. And that's exactly what she did to me. She convinced my grandmother that I was an unfit parent in order to find a way to take my children from me just as she did my mother with my two sisters and myself.

My entire life my aunt would say to me and behind my back that I was not going to amount to anything. She also stated that I was going to wind up just like my mother, strung out on drugs and would only be good for laying on my back. I felt she hated me the most because of her sister, my mother's actions in the past. It was a normal routine for me to feel the wrath of my mother's curses from my entire family and my aunt's messy ways.

47

I will never forget the day my aunt convinced my grandmother to put me out the home when she did not agree with me going out enjoying life whenever I felt the need. This irritated her to a degree of sabotaging my relationship with my grandmother and my children. My grandmother being used by my aunt agreed to put me out in the cold with my children. With nowhere else to go, I asked my next-door neighbor if I could stay with her and her granddaughter who had two small children until I found an apartment for my family and she agreed. My children would visit grandmother's home every day being that we were only next door to her.

It seemed as if nothing had changed except for where we slept at night. I was putting things in place to move to Wisconsin where my dad, the man who stepped in to help raise me, resided. All was moving along well in my eyes until the evening came where I had to leave my children with the neighbor's grandmother and her young grandchildren. I was almost out of diapers for my daughter so I needed to go to the store which was four blocks away from the home. The young lady and I walked to the store, purchased pampers and returned to the house where I was greeted with chaos. Her grandmother informed me my family had watched me leave and as I left they attempted to come to her home and take my children without my knowledge. My aunt and grandmother told the neighbor they saw me leave in a car with a man. They also said they could hear my children crying and being spanked. I asked the neighbor did she spank my children and she replied no she did not. She said what my family heard was my friend's youngest son crying because he was sleepy and ready for bed. I went to my children and asked them if they were they okay and did anyone harm them. They replied, "Mommy we are okay, no one did anything to us. Grandma and auntie came over screaming and yelling trying to take us." I comforted my children and told them everything would be fine. We laid down for the night watching a movie and eventually falling asleep.

As I awakened the next morning to my astonishment, one of my older female cousins was beating on the neighbor's front door. She was banging on the windows and door yelling, "Tiffany if you don't come out of there with those kids and give them to grandma I am going to kick the door in, come get them out of there, then beat your ass. I'll be back in ten minutes so you better make your decision." My oldest female cousin was the ring leader and is the one my aunt and grandmother calls when they have a problem with someone in the family. This cousin will either scare the crap out of someone or physically jump on them. My cousin came back ten minutes later banging on the door once again. She said, "Come on out or I'm coming in and when I do, I'm going to mess you up." To keep her from kicking the neighbor's door in I stepped out of the house. She instantly grabbed me around the throat choking me and leaning me over the highest point of the porch to throw me over to the ground. She screamed while causing a scene, "You have five minutes to hand my baby cousins over to your grandmother and leave them there so she can raise them." At that moment, I felt

50

helpless and hopeless. I felt as though I had no other option than to do as I was told or she would kill me like she had threatened to do. It was no secret the type of person she was. I gathered my children and their belongings and walked them to my grandmother's home. My aunt, another female cousin and oldest sister were in the living room waiting to jump on me. My grandmother and I sat down in the living room and began to talk. She explained to me that she did not want to take my children from me and she only wanted to take care of them while I got myself together and, on my feet, financially. I totally understood her position and wanted more for the lives of my children. I felt as though I was leaving them in the safest place possible. My cousin and grandmother then had me write a letter stating that I was giving my children to grandmother temporarily until I could afford to care for them financially the way she saw fit. Grandmother and I both signed and dated the letter. She needed to make sure I signed it in order to gain assistance from the government to care for my children. I sat with my children and explained to them that I would be back for them and that I needed to get myself in order for them. We all cried in pain for we knew we would be separated for a long period of time. The pain on my baby's face crushed my heart. They did not want me to leave and neither did I. I held my children tightly not wanting to let go but I knew eventually I had to release them. I walked them to the kitchen, kissed them one last time and vanished. I relocated the next morning and headed out for my new beginning and fresh start at life in Wisconsin. That was going to be the hardest task of my life, living without my children. God please help me...

"My children will get an education even if I don't have but one dress to put on."

Bernice McMurray Scott-

52

-Cycles of Resilience-

Ch. 6

Transformers: Abductors in Disguise

Moving to a small city in Wisconsin was the goal to start fresh and new. There was my new apartment; car and all seemed perfect for the most part despite not having my children with me. I worked a third shift job in a warehouse packaging your global air fresheners and candles. I initiated the development of friendly relationships with a few of my co-workers. I gravitated in conversations with a gentleman who was intellectually brilliant. A good looking African American man was something I familiarized with. This man stood six feet three inches tall with long black wavy hair and weighed roughly two hundred thirty pounds. We conversed hours at a time engaging in an array of topics such as family orientation, the governmental system, and interactions of multiple ethnic groups, racism and so forth. Not once did the subject of God and the spirit of the divine come about. As the nights drew longer working the overnight shift, our conversations would switch to personal affairs. He proceeded to ask if I was in a relationship with anyone. I told him I was solely focusing on having a closer relationship with God; therefore, man would have to take a backseat.

After two months lapsing of the same routine, I decided I wanted to have a gathering at my new home. I was excited of my accomplishments feeling proud of myself and my new home. I spent my hard-earned money and time on all the furnishings and sprucing so it would epitomize the uniqueness of my inner self and what my children would think of it. After weeks of planning I sent out invitations via mail delivery. I began receiving many calls from friends asking if there was anything, I needed them to bring for the party. I needed for them to show up and enjoy. As Monday approached so did another exhausting week of work. I entered the warehouse where I greeted my co-workers who I planned on inviting to my home. I passed out invitations and amongst the recipients was the gentleman I talked with for hours burning the midnight oil. As I reached to hand him his invitation he interrupts saying, "Thank you but I'm not sure if I will be able to attend." Certainly, I was disappointed for I was looking forward to spending time with him outside of the work place. We continued our nightly conversation. Two weeks passed by and its finally time to party.

At my front door sat the "key bucket." The "key bucket" is where everyone who was driving would leave their car keys so we would not experience any concern of drinking and driving accidents. I refused to have the deaths of my guests on my conscious if any of them were to leave my home and have vehicular fatalities.

There was enough food and beverages to go around three times over. The music was going, guests were arriving, food was delicious and my guests were having a wonderful time. All were getting to know one another, dancing in full affect and all was well. As the night progressed, more alcohol was consumed and food was depleting. It was two o'clock in the morning and guests were beginning to sober up and return to their cars. I went into my room to retrieve the "key bucket" for those guests who I felt could drive home safely. For other guests who were not capable of driving I suggested they sleep it off. Roughly about six or seven guests slept off their liquor after napping for a while. I returned to my bedroom to get their car keys and let them out. I noticed there was one person who was still in a drunken state and sleep on my living room floor. I did not disturb his rest and I went back to my bedroom closed my door and fell off to sleep.

Stunned! I was awakened in excruciating pain, someone was beating me on my back with wire hangers. Lash after lash screaming and hollering from the terrible pain as though I was a slave. I didn't realize who was beating me until I rolled over and saw his face. I would not have Imagined it was the same man I would spend countless hours talking with at work. My crush had transformed into a monster from hell. He dropped the hangers he had extended to look and feel like whips and began punching me with his fists. I cried out to him, "Please stop! Why are you doing this to me? I thought I knew you! How could you do this?" I then prayed that he stopped hitting me. The next words out of his mouth was, "Put some hoe clothes on and get outside and make my money bitch! You belong to me now and no one can do anything about it." I pleaded to him to please leave me alone. He punched me in the chest so hard that I flew across my bedroom into a corner and slide down the wall where I stayed balled in the fetal position crying. He marched toward me saying, "Bitch get up and shut the hell up. You're my whore now." As I stood, I was afraid that he might hit me again so I did what he told me to do. I gathered my thoughts and put on a pair of jeans and sweat shirt. He says, "Take that shit off. Put on the freakiest shortest thing you have." I pretended like I could not find anything that fit that description of clothing. He went through my dresser drawers and found a tank top, mini skirt and a pair of fish net stockings. He threw the clothes at me and said, "Bitch put this on and hurry up. You have money to make for Daddy." While putting on my clothes I reached for my phone while he was getting my car keys. As I was dialing for emergency assistance, he entered the room, snatching the phone from my hand and said, "You're trying to call the police bitch. They can't help you. You'll be dead before they get here if you pull that shit again." I yelled, "Okay, I won't do it anymore just don't kill me." He grabbed my jacket and two pairs of high heels and forced me out of my home at gun point. We proceeded to walk to my car where he opened the driver door and told me to get in. He said, "Climb over the seat and if you try to escape, I'll shoot you dead." I did exactly what he said once again. He put the car in drive and pulled off. I never seen or been back to that home again. My life no longer belonged to me and I felt not one of my friends or family members would look for me, let alone put out a missing person report for me for they had discarded me as a human being. I was yet again trapped in another world I had known anything of.

After an hour or so of driving lapsed, we parked on the side of a burgundy three-story house that sat on the corner of the street. We walked to the side entrance of the house where there were cameras to see who came in and who went out. He rang the doorbell and a man came to the door and said, "Looks like you've got a good money maker for us this time pimping." I was then forced into the world of human trafficking becoming a sex slave and a prostitute. They discussed if they should take me to the top floor of the house or to the basement where they keep all the other victimized women and young girls. They chose to take me upstairs. We started walking up to the top floor and once that door was opened, I immediately knew I was in a pimp's palace and a whore house. I was met by a woman well in her late sixties and her pimp who had to be in his early eighty's. She sat me down and immediately explained the rules of sex trafficking. She shared a bit of her story with me on how she got into sex slavery and how she had enjoyed it well over 40 years. It was one of the saddest and humiliating stories I'd heard but she seemed very proud of being a prostitute. After hearing her explain the game she instructed me on what was to come next. She said, "It's time for an examination of your body and what your best sexual positions are." I refused to comply with her request to show her and the men present my sexual acts and having to engage with the eighty-year-old man. She slapped me with the back of her hand. Hitting the floor bleeding from the nose and mouth I heard, "Let's give her something from the tray. That should help calm this whore down." When the tray was displayed to me there were all types of pills and cocaine on it. They decided to give me three pills and forced me to swallow them. I fell into a slumber and when I came to, I was completely naked. I had been raped. My abductor then escorted me down to the basement where there were nine other women and young girls.

The basement was called "The Dungeon." A dark cold cemented room with no windows or any way to escape. There was an unbearable stench of blood floating in the atmosphere. I felt nothing but darkness, heartache and death coming from the dungeon. Seeing the grieving women ranging in age from seventeen to thirty was agonizingly pitiful for me and now I had become one of them. My heart ached as I listened to the stories of the women. They all had been kidnapped, beaten, raped, drugged and emotionally abused. Nor did they feel as though any of their family members would be looking for them. We all had a few things in common; our families abandoned us. Our parents were drug addicts or left us at young ages to raise ourselves or by other family members who didn't have the time to care for us in the manner we needed. My heart wept for us ladies all night long.

I cried while men were sent down to choose which one of us, they wanted for their own wicked sexual pleasures as they bargained the prices with our abductors and pimps. That night I was not chosen due to my initiation of rape and the bruising on my face and body. It wasn't appealing for the pimps to send us with a client and/or "john" wounded because that was bad for business.

I continuously prayed to the Creator asking him to forgive me for all the wrong I had done to people and to help me and the other girls and women out of this beastly hell hole. I felt as though my prayers were unanswered and God was disappointed with me and left me all alone to suffer. I drowned into a deep depression and I did not know how to come out of it nor did I feel worthy enough to be saved.

For the next twelve months, I was sold repeatedly, pimped, raped, drugged, beaten, choked, spit on and left for dead on more occasions than I can count. Twelve hours a day for one year I was exploited and sold to the highest bidding pervert. The brainwashing, mental manipulation, spiritual manipulation and everything in between was reason enough to attempt suicide every chance I obtained. Over time, I became accustomed to the mistreatment and imprisonment. I felt like my pimp was the only person who seemed to love and care for me. I grew into defending him at all times at whatever cost. Acting in the manner of defending this man the way I did forced me think about why I would run away from things my entire life.

Being a coward and not facing whatever the situation head on and overcoming that particular fear. Most of those fears were finding me and I was terrified of what I would become. Terrified because of my past and the things people would say about me. Terrified that I would exceed above and beyond anything I could ever imagine. Terrified of trying my best because I thought my best would not be good enough. Terrified that I would turn out to be just like my mother; strung out and never there for my children. Terrified that I would have to face myself every day and choose to do one of two things; lie to myself and make it through the day or tell myself the truth about who I had become. I became extremely angry with myself. I was angry that I allowed many men to penetrate me even though I knew better. I didn't forget the lessons I was taught as a child but I did wash them from my memory to have whatever I wanted to suit my need for more sex.

Sex was my ultimate addiction. Without sex, I felt worthless and was afraid to be alone with myself because I knew without sex, I had nothing. Sex was an everyday practice in my life. As the saying goes, practice makes perfect and I was able to perfect my craft as if it was a regular job working eight hours a day.

I was in the sex trade for twelve months and it felt like a lifetime. I stayed in because I felt like I had nowhere else to go. No one would accept me for who I was. No one understood me and I wasn't sure if I wanted to change according to what people thought I should be. There were many times I could have escaped from the sex trade but I didn't want to. I was finally in a world where I was accepted by everyone because I had a vagina in between my legs. It wasn't something that I had to read. It wasn't a pop quiz test in school that I had to study for. It wasn't memorizing lines for a play I didn't want to be involved in. It wasn't about making someone else feel proud of me. It was about tricking men into believing I was their dream girl and fulfilling that title for them. I had a challenge in front of me and I knew there was no way I would lose because the challenge was already a part of me. It came packaged in a tiny box and the only way you could receive your gift was if you had

65

the coin to insert into the slot machine; pull the handle and see if you had a match. If the cherries weren't lined in a row you lost and continued to feed the machine until you finally won. The more money you added the more gifts you could unwrap.

I stayed in human trafficking because I thought the only way to feel love was through the penis and vagina or just having someone to be next to; I with their anatomy mixed with mine. I stayed in because I knew I could satisfy someone really well and for me that was a major accomplishment. I wanted to feel proud and accomplish something for the first time in my life. I didn't realize how much I had already accomplished simply by being there for someone if they needed a shoulder to cry on. The simple things... I stayed in because I truly did not want to leave. I did not know how to adjust to the world outside of those four walls and was not willing to find out. I didn't know if I would be accepted by anyone because not only was I kidnapped but I was now tainted with smoke fires from the loins of a man's hell and I liked it. I liked it because it liked me and they found satisfaction with being inside my essence. I stayed because I was tired of running away from me. I was tired of having to face my ugly truths and then having to disclose them with others. What did I look like sharing with people that I was a sex addict and not by choice? I would have been a damn fool to exploit myself. I didn't want to lay all my cards on the table for everyone to see. However, I laid my "muffin" on the table for everyone to see and I was content. The devil had me and nothing could keep me from him. It didn't matter what was happening to me I had turned into a monster. God no longer existed in me, for I felt He never answered my cries and was ashamed of the person I had turned out to be.

"Everything will change. The only question is growing up or decaying."

-Nikki Giovanni-

Ch. 7

The Grace of God

But there came a time when the spirit of God wouldn't give up on me. My life had purpose but I could not see it because of the darkness. The late-night whispers of my grandfather and great aunt speaking words of encouragement saying, "Don't give up now baby. God is not done with you yet. Hold on just a little while longer." They flashed pictures of my life in the church serving the Creator and what was to come in my future life. As my eyes were closed, I could see a beam of light shining ever so brightly. With all the words of wisdom being shared with me from my ancestors, I still wanted at the same time to be taken from this earth and out of my misery. I was ready to die! This seemed like the only way I was going to escape from a treacherous life of lies and death haunting me. I prayed for help asking the Creator to deliver me from the evilness that was holding me hostage. It was like an emotional roller coaster I could not get off. I was locked in my own self and ready to self-destruct. The more I prayed the stronger my faith was getting yet I was weakened physically and mentally. I heard my children calling me to come home one dreary evening. Their voices saying, "Mommy, where are you? We miss you! We love you! We need you!" I believe that was the only thing that kept me from killing me; the spirit of my grandfather, my great aunt and my children calling for me to come home. I eventually gained the strength to fight through and fight my way out of severe depression. The more I was illegally exploited the harder I prayed for a way out.

Months passing, my pimp and I eventually traveled to different cities where he would sell me at truck stops, motels and fairly deserted areas for hours even days at a time and he was present everywhere I was. I remember traveling to a small town in southern Illinois. We arrived at an apartment complex and were greeted at the door by an older woman. He embraced her with a hug and kiss. I overheard her say to him, "My son, I'm so happy to see you. It's been a very long time. You look good son." He introduced me to his mother as his girlfriend. He stepped away for a short moment and I pleaded to her for help. I informed her I had been kidnapped by her son. She said to me, "Bow down to him bitch and get in line because you are his slave. You have no opinions or thoughts. Just do as you are told and you will live. Stay in a hoes place." I could not believe the words she was saying to me. She then told me she was and has been a "bottom bitch" since she was sixteen. She had been pimped out and sold by her husband for many years. All I could do was shake my head in shame and pray to God to rescue me before something even more terrifying and tragic happened such as my death. She explained to me all the men in her family were pimps. After some time in this town of being pimped, poked and prodded we drove back to Wisconsin where I was in the driver's seat.

I was driving on I-94 and had the strangest feeling in the pit of my stomach. It was a feeling of anxiety, confusion and the unknown. My abductor was in the passenger's seat sleep.

I began looking around on the expressway noticing that there were quite a few of unmarked detective cars surrounding me. I remember looking down at my phone and looking back up to the road and not seeing anyone. It seemed as though they all disappeared. I continued driving for another twenty minutes, seeing my exit and merged to the right to exit the expressway.

As I drove up the ramp, he woke up from sleeping and told me to pull into a parking lot of a hotel. I was curious in knowing if this would be another stop for me to be sold. There were about four hotels in the vicinity. He went inside one of the hotels, paid for one room and came back outside to me waiting in the car. While he was in the hotel office paying for the room, I noticed that everyone had vacated from the parking lots and restaurants nearby. It was a bit strange to me so I sat there in the car not knowing what to do. As he resurfaced and gave me the key for the room, police and sheriffs arrived surrounding the car. My pimp jumped out of the car running like a track and field superstar making a mad dash crossing the expressway below us to escape. The officers chased him until they caught him two miles away. The police said the only way they knew where he was located was from following his foot prints in the snow.

Meanwhile, I'm standing next to the car in handcuffs being read my Miranda rights for a crime I did not commit. I did not know why I was being placed under arrest. I explained to the officers that I had been kidnapped from my home and that man forced me into prostitution and other sexual acts. I began weeping knowing that my prayers were finally answered. I screamed, "God you did not forget about me when everyone else did." I'll never forget the look on the officer's face. He was stunned asking, "Are you serious?" I said, "Yes, officer and it's been the worst time of my life." I was transferred to another squad car and escorted to the police station where I called my eldest sister's dad and told him what happened to me. As we talked on the phone, he seemed very happy to know that I was safe. He then said, "You're okay, but I'm not coming to get you out of jail for whatever you did. I don't get anyone out of jail." I simply wanted to let him know I was safe and alive. The officer who saved me took me into an interrogation room and began to take my statement on what occurred. I explained to him everything I had been through. He asked if I remembered where I had been held hostage. I said yes but I didn't know the address but I remembered how to get there. I gave him the pimps name and they ran him in their database and noticed he had recently been released from prison on the charges of armed robbery of financial institutions. He was released from prison right before I met him. You never truly know a person when you are not listening to the spirit you were created with. I remained in the custody of the police for twenty-four hours until all of my details on what occurred came back positive. After going to court, the judge ordered the man who abducted me to nine years in federal prison for armed robbery and not kidnapping. The judicial system has yet again failed another person who was abducted, pimped and made to become a sex slave against their will. It's time to move on with my life, again!

"If I could have convinced more slaves that they were slaves, I could have freed thousands more."

-Harriet Tubman-

Ch. 8

There is No Place Like Home

I was left with the broken pieces of my life to put together after my release from jail and freedom from sex slavery. I was far from getting *myself in order*. I visited my oldest sister's father's home to borrow some money. I wanted to go to Chicago to see my children. I was in desperate need to see them and I was immensely grateful for the *few dollars* dad had given me.

My next stop was to my cousin's house. My cousin was dad's nephew who lived about ten minutes away. I knocked on his front door and my knock was answered. He gave me a huge embrace full of love; the type that I needed.

"Where have you been cousin?" He asked. "I've missed you," he added before I could say anything.

I sat down at his kitchen table and explained to him what I had recently endured. The expression on his face was of devastation and anger and he wanted to seek revenge on my abductor. I was trying to move forward with life, so I quickly changed the subject.

We joined the guys who were watching a late football game on the couch. One of the men I had never seen before my abduction. I introduced myself and asked his name and where was he originally from. He had a very thick accent. He said he was from Pennsylvania and had recently moved to Wisconsin. He told me that I was very beautiful and he would like to see me once I returned from Chicago. I told him I would think about it. He said if you do, "I'll be waiting here for you."

My cousin let me stay at his apartment that night. Early the next morning, I rose before the crack of dawn to take the Metra train to Chicago. The hour and a half train ride felt slow and quick at the same time. And my thoughts about my life were like the fast passing trees. We snaked through the old industrial parts of Illinois. It was like a past life full of promise and now full of too many doubts. Then we zoomed through the prairie fields, and again it was like a metaphor of life. This time reminding me about moving fast and if that crashes, the momentum shatters life into many broken pieces. So, we kept going, and I had finally arrived at Ogilvie Transportation Center in Chicago. I took two "L" trains and three buses to get to grandmother's home on the southside of Chicago.

I finally arrived at granny's front door and rang the bell. She peeped through the side window and saw it was me. When she opened the door, I embraced her with arms wide open and she said it was good to see me. I returned the sentiment: "Granny, I've missed you and I thank you for taking care of my children and for protecting them." Then I asked to see them. She told me they were upstairs in their bedrooms. My sisters and I slept in those same rooms when were children. Before us, my mom and her six siblings grew up in those rooms as well. I am sure that there were plenty memories in the two attic bedrooms. The rooms were small and could only hold two twin size beds, two dressers, a coat rack and a black and white television.

Grandma summoned my children downstairs to the main floor. My oldest daughter walked in grandmother's room, looked at me and did not say anything. She turned to grandma and asked, "Who is that?" My heart shattered into a million pieces. The pain was still in my heart when I replied: "My sunshine, how are you?"

She said, "Mommy is that you?"

I replied, "Yes, my baby, It's me."

She ran to me and jumped in my lap and kissed me all over my face. And the pain was forgotten with each kiss It felt like medicine. She then ran as fast as she could to get her brother. My son walked into the room and transformed from doubt to joy. He said, "Mommy, please don't leave me again. I need you always and forever."

Then the tears came to my eyes as I held him like a sudden rainstorm. I reminded him that I loved him and nothing could ever keep me away from him. That was my sincere hope. I explained to him that I hit a few bumps in the road, but the journey was not over yet. I still had work to do; *to get myself in order.*

"Son, you have the spirit of God within you. Never worry about anything. I will never be "Apart" from you because I am and will forever be "A Part" of you." He nodded his head in agreement with me.

I turned to grandmother and asked about my baby girl. When I was forced to leave my children, my youngest child was only a few months old. My grandmother said that my baby was in my uncle's room.

I walked into his room and saw the most amazingly beautiful child and she was mine. *God is great!* I picked her up and she looked at me as if she remembered me. She looked like, "Who is this and where has she been?" And I tried not to give her the answer that was lurking in my soul. I reached back to the joyful side of my mind and said to her with my soul, *it is good to see you.* And like this we communicated and were grateful to be back together.

Grandmother allowed me to stay the entire day. She would not allow me to spend the night in her home with my children because I had to *get myself in order*, even though, there were many challenges ahead of me. So, we had ice cream and cake and sang "happy birthday" to my oldest daughter and I left again.

"I have discovered in life that there are ways of getting almost anywhere you want to go, if you really want to go."

-Langston Hughes-

-Cycles of Resilience-

Ch. 9

The Way of Habit

Ay! The way things were unfolding was life changing and grim, but I still had to make a go of it. I was back in Wisconsin; back at my cousin's apartment and back to looking for a job.

As the days passed I grew closer to my cousin's roommate. He was handsome and charming and he made sure I was comfortable. He seemed genuine and so, we started dating. The relationship started as a wonderful friendship and he allowed me to be me in his presence. We hung out when we were not working. He introduced me to football and I instantly became a fan of his hometown team. Things seemed to be looking up, however, there were some mountains to climb.

I was trying to deal with my abduction internally, as I thought I didn't need to seek psychiatric or medical attention. I figured I could fix myself. Plus, I was ashamed and

84

embarrassed to discuss the frightening details of my personal issue's with sexual exploitation. He was dealing with problems that had chased him away from home, to a place where we would forget about the past and focus on the two of us. I wanted to deal with my demons through Christ. And he was willing to follow the ways of the God, even though he was a Muslim.

We discussed going to church together. He was open to going for my sake, though that was not his "forte." He said, he had promised himself never to step foot in another church again, because he had been burnt by the church before.

We both had issues with our families, yet there was no way to resolve any of those complicated burdens. We did what we could and we focused on each other. We called it LOVE. Our version of love was based on not knowing the truth. I was not supposed to ask any questions about family history, especially the loss of his mom and his relationship with his children's mother. If I did, there were no answers.

Another year ended and another approached, then he asked for my hand in marriage. I secretly hoped for a fairy tale proposal: a nice speech about our LOVE; then the kneeling; and finally, a beautiful ring. Of course, it didn't happen that way. The proposal was his response to being caught with another woman. My boyfriend had been cheating on me for a very long time and I knew it, but had never caught him in the act. I finally did one day after work. I arrived home from work before he did. And later in the evening I saw him being dropped off in a SUV by someone, that I presumed to be his girlfriend. Actually, he was driving the truck. I instantly became enraged and left the apartment instead of blowing up on him. However, I asked him to go back to his gift bearing girlfriends and leave me alone. I went for a long walk which lasted roughly an hour and a half. I cooled down and went back home.

I was attempting to eat dinner when he asked me to go look in the closet in the bedroom. I did and found an envelope on which he had written his proposal. "Will you marry me please? P.S. I'm serious." That was my proposal.

Reluctantly, I accepted even though I had reservations. I was apprehensive because I had not really addressed my experience as a young person who had been kidnapped and sexually exploited. My family life in Chicago was broken: my mother, my granny, and my children were all calling my name in the spirit. I suggested that he and I seek couple's counseling. His response was "no one can tell me about myself especially when they don't even know me." That was one of the craziest things I had ever heard. I reached out to a minister who I knew personally. He agreed to counsel us for free, but that too fell on deaf ears. Maybe we could fix this in the marriage, so I went along with the engagement. Everything felt abnormal. I was a nervous wreck. And on our wedding day, we went to the courthouse without our families.

Then the judge called our names and the pangs of doubt knotted in my stomach like a solid knot of premonition. But, the hope for love and my own family conquered my apprehension. We oddly danced toward matrimony.

I lifted hope like an olive branch and I danced toward love. I said let me love like the old folks used to do; like my grandpa and grandma. I said to myself, let us dance for the children yet unborn; let us dance for the joy yet to come and let us dance for the love that we need. So, I answered the judge's questions. I looked into his eyes for the sign of our love and I was met with mystery. The judge called my name and I answered. I put down my name in the book of matrimony and I was going to give it a good go.

As we stood on the front steps of the courthouse, I asked my husband, "Husband, what were you thinking when we were saying our vows?" He said, "I was thinking about fried chicken. I'm hungry. Are you going to cook?"

I did not like his answer and my heart fell to the floor. I felt like our relationship and marriage was a joke to him and I wanted to slap him in the face at that very moment. I felt alone and embarrassed. My natural instinct was to turn right around, run quickly back to the judge and get our marriage annulled.

No! He is the only one I got and he is my husband now. I took a deep breath and decided to be a good wife like my grandma was to grandpa. I waited on him hand and foot. We went home to our new house where I prepared a five-course meal for him since that was what he wanted for his matrimonial treat.

I took care of all his needs as a wife should for her husband. I spared no effort in making sure that we were building a solid unit. And I supported him in his career, his emotional development, his children and extended family.

Our honeymoon was not a full moon when I began feeling lonely. I needed him much more than he could be available. I knew I also wanted to pursue my dream as a fashion model. He could not give me the support I needed. I began to drift into myself and I stopped caring about his feelings.

We eventually decided that Wisconsin was not the place where we wanted to live out the rest of our lives together. He decided that we could either move to North Carolina or Georgia.

"You can be the lead in your own life."

-Kerry Washington-

-Cycles of Resilience-

Ch. 10

Deep in the Rabbit Hole

The sweet smell of pine welcomed us to Atlanta. It was the smell of freedom and fortune. They say that the sense of smell is our oldest sense; the first to develop. It is there to soothe us; to orient us in space; and to protect us. And the scientists say that our sense of smell is responsible for most of our behavior as biological systems. So, the pines of Georgia welcomed us. I prayed that *the goodness and mercy of the Lord would follow us.*

Soon after settling in, my husband started looking for work. He found a security job in one of the many night clubs of Atlanta. His job required him to be absent on most evenings and he slept most of the

day time. I felt idle and without purpose. And the desire to pursue my own career became acute.

I wanted to be a high fashion model ripping all the runways that I walked. I loved modeling because of the many transformations that were possible. I could become a new person with makeup and wardrobe changes. The makeup will even cover all my freckles and blemishes to make me look flawless on the outside. However, I felt ugly and shamed on the inside.

Walking the runway was cathartic for me. Every step I took was a stomp on those who have hurt me. Each step helped me crush their souls. Ay! Walking on the runway helped me release my anger that was swelling in me. But that did not help. The more I crushed my nemesis on the runway, the more the anger and disappoint of my life grew. And soon I was in a full-blown depression. I was on a pathological treadmill with short periods of joy and longer periods of sadness.

My husband did not want to entertain my concern for the deadly cycle we were planting for ourselves. I could not take any more of his selfish acts and I pushed him to the back burner. That led him to step out of our marriage on several occasions. He established emotional and sexual relationships with women at the various night clubs where he worked. I found most of the evidence on our home computer and I confronted him and I wanted out.

And he got angry: "I see why so many men have beaten you. You deserved every bit of it," he said. When he said that I got angry too and the whole argument escalated into a physical altercation. But I still forgave him.

We were conducting life on our own without a village to intercede into our "foolishness." I knew I needed Christ. I started going to church on Sundays. And I tried to encourage him to go with me. Sundays would have been difficult for him because he worked on most Saturday nights. But we had to do something to help us live an emotionally healthy life. And there was no cooperation coming from him. Instead, I was met with more abuse. So, I asked for a divorce.

He was standing in the bathroom when I uttered to him: "I want a divorce from you. You are not the kind, loveable, joyful, encouraging, spiritually compassionate person you used to be. You are very argumentative, hateful and you have such a negative spirit with a [very] aggressive temper and it's out of control. You've hurt me too many times and I do not love you anymore. I'm leaving you and I want a divorce as soon as possible."

Before I could catch my breath, he took off his wedding band and threw it in my face.

"Bitch! I hate you!" he said while charging at me. "I'm going to beat your ass like every other man has. I see why everyone hates you." As he was charging toward me, I tried to turn around to run down the hallway. Before I could make my move, he reached for me and pushed me to the ground. He kicked and stomped me as if I were a man. He placed all his weight over me. It looked like a six-foot five demon standing over me. And his weight was no less than two hundred and thirty-five pounds. He was trying to kill me. I asked God to give me the strength to stand up and fight. The last experience taught me to fight back. *I fought back*. As I laid on the floor facing him, I started to kick towards him frantically trying to prevent him from picking me up. I landed a kick to his chest which made him stumble backward. I jumped up, ran to the kitchen and picked up a butcher knife.

"Please, stay away. I will kill you if you come any closer to me. Step back and let me leave this house."

His aunt who had been watching the fight finally asked him to allow me to leave. And she asked him to go to his room and cool off. And he did. I quickly ran to the neighbor's house and called the police. Our marital bliss was short lived and ended with a police report.

"I have learned over the years that when one's mind is made up, this diminishes fear; knowing what must be done does away with fear."

-Rosa Parks-

-Cycles of Resilience-

Ch. 11

The Incubus

Incubus:

1.) A male demon believed to have sexual intercourse with women during their sleep.

2.) A cause of distress and anxiety.

3.) A nightmare.

The move out of the home I shared with my ex-husband was emotionally draining, heart breaking and exhausting. However, I moved on with my life in my studio apartment. Each traumatic experience was like a school – "the school of hard knocks " I learned to fight back incubuses, I learned to leave with myself at an affordable cost; and I learned to purse my own goals.

The telephone calls for modeling rolled in tidal waves and I was booked for several fashion events and the largest fashion show of my career so far. And I was so fortunate that I was able to book eleven out of the thirteen designers that I wanted to work with. I also had the opportunity to work and learn from one of the world's legendary and iconic female models. What an amazing experience and blessing to be in the graces of my career role models.

After the big show, we went to cocktail hour where a well put together fella grasped my attention. He stood six-feet and five inches tall and weighed roughly close to three hundred pounds. And I saw him as a protector. That should keep my ex away. However, I was still carrying on with the same pattern: a physically imposing man, good-looking man, turning over affection to them even before they asked; and looking for a protector and physical desire. I did not investigate what type of man he was; whether he was a demon or not, or whether he preyed on women or prayed to God with sincerity. He was really the first man to give me any attention after I left my ex. I was also desiring the touch of a man that essentially ended after the first year of marriage to my ex-husband.

With my mindset, I became the facilitator and sashayed toward him and seductively introduced myself. *The goose was cooked.* And I also knew he wouldn't resist the temptation of my sex appeal. I also was not able to resist his close-up appeal. He was charismatic and stylish from head to toe.

We had a short conversation and exchanged telephone numbers and decided to meet for breakfast a few days later. We dated for a while and as the months moved on, I started to spend the night at his place frequently. And I felt perfectly peaceful. And I grew even closer to him. I began spending so much time at his house than my own. Eventually, he professed his LOVE for me and asked me to move in.

Things were good at first, but then I saw characteristics in him that I had seen in men previously. He was possessive like the two men before him and perhaps even others. He wanted things done in his way. He wanted me to dress a certain way. He wanted to control every aspect of me. And he would take me around his family and friends and display me as his "little model girl."

I did not always like this and I began to push back and the verbal abuse started about the slightest difference in preference. He wanted his dinner at 6:30pm, promptly, every day. I would encore his wrath if I was two minutes late delivering his food from the second-floor kitchen to the first-floor bedroom. He would yell insanities and throw full childlike temper tantrums. I was wandering: *what is it about people and control? Why does it matter if I am two minutes late to prepare dinner? Where is your sense of gratitude? My pimp was like that and so was my ex-husband. And now this? Um uhm! What is wrong with me?*

I decided to move out and he must had known because he had devised his own plan to keep me hostage. He rigged the front door and the garage so that I was not able to open them without his permission or while he was at work.

I heard a voice in my head that said: "You are going to die here and no one will ever know where you are." I panicked and began scheming my get away plan. The last time this happened to me I did not know where I was. I knew I was psychologically unwilling to get away and like the elephants who are chained to a tree and get accustomed to it, so was I to that pimp house; like any other animal that is conditioned to be controlled, so was I. But not this time.

After he went to work, I hatched my get-a-way plan. I ran from the front door to the upstairs where there was a balcony. I swung the door open, walked out to the balcony, looked and contemplated jumping down to the ground. I was sure that my bones would not endure the fifty-foot drop. I would undoubtedly break a few bones or worse. And no one would probably notice just as the neighbors did not know all those girls lived in a whore house at the dead end of the street.

I went back to the living room and called my girlfriend in Wisconsin. I stayed on the phone and continued the conversation about escaping until he came home for lunch. I told my friend that I was trapped in his house.

"Why did you not call the police?" she asked.

"Well, that thought never crossed my mind," I answered.

Surprisingly, he snatched the phone out of my hand, threw it into the fireplace where it shattered. He picked me up off the couch; carried me to the bedroom, ripped my clothes off and raped me. Then he smoked a marijuana joint and raped me again. This time there was blood raging out of my own vagina. He then rolled another joint and forced me to smoke it. *I have met this demon before. This is a reincarnation.* He made me submerge myself in water so the bleeding would stop. Afterward, he made me go to work with him and the rape and the smoking became some sort of demonic ritual. He made me follow him everywhere; to work, the grocery store, and to see his friends.

And the devil revisited me in my sleep. His ways are vile and merciless. He stunned me and said to me, "it's time for you to die and join me."

I asked, "Why?"

And he replied, "You were cheating on me. I was standing in the corner watching you!"

The slap woke me up and I could not believe what was happening.

"In my dream you cheated on me and I saw you!" the incubus said.

What?

And he began having delusional conversations with his imaginary sentinel about my conduct and my infidelity to him. They must've been telling him the truth, but he would not believe them. And that got him further enraged. It was like in "The Wizard of Oz." He got so angry with the voices in his head, that he started to run away. He ran into the bedroom drywall,

104

then into the closet drywall, and into the shower where he ran into formidable opposition of the shower's glass door.

I ran for my bible and prayed. I prayed that God would release the demonic forces that had taken control over him. I also prayed for God to spare my life. Then I heard loud stomping sounds coming back into the bedroom. He must have seen the bible and said, "God can't save you from me." He placed in his hands his grandmother's bible. His grandmother worshipped demons. He made me kneel to his feet and pray to him. He stood over me with his arms to his sides and his palms facing the floor. He was still talking to his demons about me. He went and retrieved his grandmother's "blessed oil" and poured it all over my body. Then he instructed me to stand up. And I stood. He instructed me to sit on the bed. And I did. He went back to the closet to frantically retrieve something. When he returned, he had a gun in his hand.

I instantaneously screamed, "Please don't kill me. I don't want to die. I'm sorry. Please don't do this to me."

"Shut up! Shut the fuck up! I will get you now for all that you have done to me."

He sat on the bed next to me turning the gun on himself. He opened his mouth, placed the gun in it, with his right finger on the trigger. I yelled, "No, don't do it." He removed the gun out of his mouth and said, "If that's how you want it, I will use it on you. I'm not playing with you. I'm going to kill you." He grabbed my face tightly with his left hand and said, "Open wide bitch." While clinching my mouth tighter and tighter, he shoved the gun in my mouth and said, "It's time for you to go to hell. You first, then I'm coming to meet you there because that's my home."

Finger on the trigger with red eyes and without a soul, he was about to take my life. I muffled to him, "I have children, don't kill me. I have to live for them." I don't know what came over him but he slowly withdrew the pistol from my mouth as I was praying to God that He stopped this man from killing me. He said, "I'm not going to kill you now but just know I will if you ever do anything to me again. I am the almighty satan. You will do as I tell you. You will worship me and only me." He instructed me to lie down next to him and go to sleep.

I laid down and closed my eyes as if I were asleep. In that moment I prayed that God watched over me for the night and that he would spare my life yet again. At one point, I could feel this man that I thought I knew standing over me for a very long period of time. I didn't know what he was going to do to me. I kept my body still, ears open and focused on what I would do if he moved closer toward me. Reluctantly, he walked out of the room and headed downstairs to the basement where he remained for the rest of the night.

As morning slowly approached, I had already prepared my plan to escape. I went into an uncontrollable panic and told him I was having trouble breathing and that I needed fresh air. He opened the garage door about a half a foot, just enough for me to see daylight pouring through. I said, "open it all the way please. I need fresh air. I feel like I'm going to pass out." He honored my request and raised the door all the way. I stepped outside for the first time in weeks. As he stood at the door, I began inching down the driveway. He looked at me and in a very loud voice yelled, "You better not run on me."

I told him, "Go straight to hell." And in my sky-blue night gown and slippers to match, I ran for my life. My track and field training came back to use. I ditched my slippers and I ran like a bolt of lightning through the woods. But my brain was running ahead of my legs. I knew it would take me too long to reach the nearest fire station which was a mile down the road. I would win a foot race with him, but he had a truck and those four wheels would definitely catch up to me. So, I chose to avoid the road.

Then the spirit of God spoke to me and said, "That's the house. Go to the back door." I knocked on the door and a lady who looked to be in her mid-fifties answered the door. And asked, "Can I help you?"

My boyfriend is trying to kill me and he is running after me as we speak.

She allowed me into her home and gave me the phone to call the police.

Then she asked her daughter who was about my age to bring me a glass of water. They assured me that I would be safe and they consoled me. The mom went and called her other daughter and to my surprise the girls were twins. The girls both "laid hand on me." They began to describe what they saw around me; two angels. One of the twins said, "They are always with you." And I finally began to calm down. "The police are at your house right now," she added. And she went on to tell me that my boyfriend has a gun pointed at the police and they have his house surrounded. It was like they were seeing everything happening at his home.

And she said the police will be here soon, "in a few seconds." Not more than one minute later the police arrived and knocked on the door. The officers asked me to accompany them back to the house that I had ran from in order to identify my boyfriend. I rode in a police car with tinted windows. We parked about twenty-five feet from the house.

I positively identified him: "Yes, officer that is him." They asked me to step outside the car to give a report. They gave me three options. I could either stay at his home, go to a friend's house or go into a shelter for battered women. I chose the shelter. As I was escorted into the house by two officers to gather my belongings, my tormenter became outraged by the sight of me. I ignored him. He professed his love for me saying, "I love you and I am so sorry. Please forgive me. Don't do this to me. I can't go back to jail. I will lose everything." I continued to ignore him. I no longer gave him any power over me. And that sent him over the moon. "I should have killed you when I had the chance." And I had my last "piece" of advice for him, "You deserve everything you have coming to you."

I retrieved my things and the police took me to the station for more questioning. Afterward, they dropped me off at a shelter for battered women.

"Faith is the black person's federal reserve system."

-Hattie McDaniel-

Ch. 12

Sheltered by Fate

While in the women's shelter, I met a lady whom I immediately connected with. We talked for hours about our situations and trying to break our toxic patterns. *But, how can one do right, when you were not taught right? The King's men know that "manners maketh man."* We reckoned that as long as I kept making the same bad choices, that I would keep having the same outcome. It was like an addiction. Only God and fate could spare me.

And, we sat to talking one day in the TV room. "There is a lady here in Atlanta who is involved with a domestic violence group, do you know of her?" my new friend asked. I knew exactly who she was talking about.

"Contact her as soon as we are finished with our discussion. This is the only way you will be able to see that God has not left your side. When you get home to Chicago you

113

are going to be reunited with your children, but it is not going to be easy for you. You will have more battles with your family in proving to them that you are worthy of your children. You will be involved in saving the lives of many children around you. No matter where you go or what you do, you will be a magnet to people who have been through what you have. It is your job, as God has instructed you, to save lives."

I listened very carefully to every word she spoke. It was essentially to *get myself in order*. It was a road unknown. Even the mental fortitude required has to come as a gift from God. I was broken and could not muster the strength and the clarity of mind to even embark on this difficult journey.

Then she continued: "You are also going to meet a gentleman..." This is where she was about to lose me. I didn't have any interest in another man right now. But I remained quiet and she continued: He "...is much older than you and he will be a minister of love. He will be pure and true to all around him. He will love you as you have searched for love your entire

114

life. He will only come once you begin doing the work of God and living in your purpose. God will reveal him right at the point of your healing breakthrough. Love him and let him guide you because God leads him."

Then she became very quiet and my brain wondered about her comments, without any coherence. It was not even clear what I may do next, if anything. What I knew for sure was that I was going to share my experiences with other women and young girls, so that they choose a better path. There was hope in her statement.

I know. I know. That is a lot she seems to be saying. Then, she on Jesus. We prayed and prayed until I started speaking in tongues." It was a language that only God and I understood.

Later on, I went into the computer room and researched my friend with the domestic violence organization and gave her a call. I was glad that she answered the phone and I told her about my situation. The following day, she called the facility and informed me that she had purchased a greyhound ticket for me to go back home to Chicago. Because in the end, "There is no place like home." I promised God that once I was back home in Chicago, I would never look back to what I had been through my entire life. I would only look back to help the next person not fall victim to such heinous crimes as I was subjected to living. As of now, I'm still living in Chicago and I can finally say I am healing and have found peace within my soul.

I have a great restorative relationship with my children and I'm married to my best friend. There is love after hate. God is love. God is hope. God is faith. God is my all and all. *LIVE.*

"I got my start by giving myself a start."

-Madame CJ Walker-

-Cycles of Resilience-

Ch. 13

Dear Mommy and Daddy

The thinking started on the greyhound bus ride back to my hometown and I had more questions than answers.

Mother, what happened to you or what forced you into your drug addiction? How did you make the choices you made? Oh Mother, why did your parents raise your children? And why were you abused by men? And about your life; did you choose the life you lived or was it forced upon you?

I do not know how your life has infested and affected my being. I can empathize with you in reference to being an outcast from your own family. I can only imagine how you felt over the course of your life. Grandmother and Grandfather did their best. They kept my mom and her siblings together. Although, some of my aunts and uncles were under other influences apart from Christ. Somehow, we became selfish; the individual became more important than the family unit as a whole and things fell apart. And pathology took over: we manipulated each other, we lied to each other, we became emotionally immature toward one another; we became materialistic, became jealous and competed against each other. We gossiped, we were vindictive and very judgmental. Imagine me throwing stones in a glass house. We did all these things, until our tight knit family was torn asunder. It was like a planetary system disintegrating and heaved all over the dark corners of space.

I was spun out of our family without the basic tools of education, self-control and deep-seated knowledge of Christ. I thought I could use my looks and manipulate my way through the abyss of this life. And I was no match for the demons I sought to impress and influence.

Living Christ-like is something we all possess for He created us all in His own image. We reflect God's own self. I refused to accept Him to be the forefront of our existence.

Mom, I have watched you as you kept things bottled inside and other times when you wanted to express yourself, but no one could understand you. They had already placed judgment upon you. You had been crucified before given the opportunity to change your ways.

I was returning to Chicago as the prodigal child. I looked at my reflection in the window of the bus and I became the woman in the mirror. Up to that time, I had never dealt with my inner most agonizing emotions. I had not asked myself the essential questions. I had not placed God at the helm of my life. As difficult as my grandparents' lives were, Christ kept their dysfunctional family together. It was a tenuous matter; he wanted to teach me a lesson as many times as necessary. The big lessons occurred in Chicago, in Milwaukee and Kenosha; and in Atlanta. And yes, I was the only constant without my Christian and Spiritual values.

The hurt you caused me. I did not stop you because I was so elated to be the baby girl thinking that you would love me. I have let you get away with manipulating me which caused me severe depression.

Dear Mother,

I forgive you for all that you did to harm me. Mother, I wondered why you had a lot of anger towards me and was even willing to take it out on me sometimes. Twice, you kicked me in the stomach and pushed me down the stairs. You did so while I was pregnant, and I kept re-playing the trauma in my head even after coming from the hospital. I almost lost my children because of your abuse. This would have caused me ruin that you wished upon me. You have said some things over the years that made me believe I was not worth anything to you or to anyone else for that matter. You said that nobody cares for me; that my sisters hate me; that your parents only wanted a chcok for my children, because they didn't love me. And that you DEFINTIELY do not LOVE me. And that you would never do shit for me. So, I got the esteem that I deserved.

You have said things like; I will never amount to anything; that no one will ever believe me, and that I was a waste of sperm. Mother, you planted a seed that you did not nurture, and I was like a wild weed instead of a cultivated flower. I cannot get your voice out of my head when you said things like; you hate the day you got pregnant with me and that you should have flushed me down the toilet. This made me feel worthless.

You said, I would be so worthless that I would only be good for laying on my back and that everyman I come across will abuse me. Your words marked my conscience like a red-hot knife and allowed your evil prophecy to come true. Oh Mother, what kind of prophet are you? You turned out to be prescient.

How would I ever succeed in life, or how would I love myself if you say you hate me? Mother, how would I embrace life if you wished to kill me and how would I not feel dumb and stupid? Don't you know mother that you are the diviner of all things good and all things bad? Mother?

Mother, you called me bad names: a bitch, a whore, and a slut. A name is everything. And you promised to beat me every chance you got until I died. And if I didn't die you wished that my children would die. Hey! This is how I know you deserve empathy. And above all, mother, you gave me away and wished my grandparents should had never retrieved me. You said I will raise myself and I did, like a snake. You said, I will go to hell; and I have been there and back. I have been beaten and raped. I have been ruined and I wished I was dead.

I did not become just like you (for a while) as you wished. I walked in your footsteps; but if not for the grace of God, I may have stayed permanently on that road. I have tried to be you and I now know your pain and I now forgive you, Mother.

Mother, I want you to know that I forgive you for all you have done to me. I forgive you in order that I will live a full life *of purpose from God. I have come to the realization that you cannot hurt me anymore.*

I am overcoming all my negative ways through the grace of God and the mercy He has spared over my life. I will be a beacon of light for my children and others to follow.........

I wish you the best in life Mommy,

I love you!

This is where my letter ended. Then I needed to write one to my dad.

Dear Daddy,

I love you and there is a void in my heart for you. I am searching high and low, near and far, crying my eyes out because...I can't see your face. I don't have a photo of you to remember our time together, if any.

I can't remember when you held me in your arms or upon your shoulders.

I do not know your voice or your smile. Do we share the same features, like my freckles? Does your heart beat or has it stopped like mine wondering where you are? I am in a panic. Daddy!

Where are you? Father, if you are out there, please know that I have searched for you. That time has now passed and I am moving on with my life. God is my Father!

I wish you luck Daddy,

I love you!

"If you don't like something, change it. If you can't change it, change your attitude."

-Maya Angelou-

Ch. 14

Family, Forgiveness and Fortitude

Dear Family,

My entire life I have lived under the assumption and persuasion to live my life to every last one of your standards. Not realizing at the time of my youth, teenage and adult years that you all were giving me the wrong direction to follow. I have spent precious years trying to imitate you all in search of finding myself. As I became old enough to start seeing things for what they were, I came to the realization that you all had your own personal agendas for my life and I became rebellious. I wanted no parts of you or to carry our family's last name. I did not feel or see an ounce of genuine unconditional love coming from you translating to me. What you all displayed was hatred and a lack of respect for one another. How majority of you bullied the next family member into giving you what you needed for your own personal needs. I've seen you all curse each other out and degrade your own blood to your friends and not bother to care how it affected the person you call your relative. I've witnessed physical altercations between most of you and we wonder why we as a family cannot come together in peace and uplift one another.

Grandfather and grandmother made sure when we all were young children we had God in our lives and made us go to church or have some form of spirituality within. Now I know for some of you it may not have been your thing, but for others it was our salvation. However, we became selfish and thought we knew everything. We figured we could do things our own way and everything would work out not realizing without the Creator of all things our "so called" lives would not be fulfilled. We have held on to family secrets that we should have shared with one another. We have lied to ourselves and on the next person with the belief that if we hold on to the hostility of our pasts, we would not be subjected to the wrath of the devil himself.

We once had a bond so tight but we all said to hell with one another, it's about me and who needs family. We think that we are immovable objects and breaking someone else down mentally and emotionally would help us gain the materialistic things the world had to offer. We carry jealousy and hatred and know that if one of us might fulfill our purpose in life, all of the hard work trying to keep them down would take the spotlight off of you. Living Christ-like is something we all possess for He created us in His own image. We are a reflection of God's own self but most of us refuse to accept Him to be the forefront of our very existence.

Our family has come to a point where we can't even pick up the telephone to see how each other is doing without harmful intentions. Most will only talk to be nosey and then gossip about that person behind their back once they've received the information they were searching for. We want things in our lives that we see others with. For example, your friend's lifestyle might be a little better than yours so you find a way to be angry with them instead of realizing that you are lacking your "true self" in the midst of your chaotic lives. Why are we holding on to the past pains we were once subjected to? We feel as though if we hold on to these things that we will overcome them. We more than likely have not tackled the issues head on and confronted the person who has harmed us. We move on as if nothing happened and live in a fairy tale land. When you do this, you keep yourself from living at your maximum potential while enjoying all the fruits of your labor. Why do we think we're better than what we are, when we have just as many issues as the next person? That's because we have a tendency of show-boating and faking the funk. We have to have the best clothes, shoes, makeup and other crap that have absolutely no meaning. We want everyone to think are lives are parfont, even though we all cry behind closed doors and sometimes forget to talk with the Creator as our tears are cleansing our minds and souls. Why do we look down upon ourselves? We look down on ourselves because we have yet to realize who you truly are. We have not tapped into our divine self. We have not sat in silence and waited on God to speak to us or direct us in what our next step in life should be.

We have fooled ourselves into thinking that we are "All-Knowing, All-Powerful" and we need no one in our lives. We blame ourselves for the harsh realities that have been set at our doorsteps. We are holding onto the things that we have no control over. We have not dealt with our inner most agonizing emotions. We believe that everyone else in the world can see us for who we are not and begin to analyze and degrade our own self. What happened to having the love of God as the forefront of our family? We tend to forget that without God on our side we have nothing. As quickly as we obtain materialistic goods, He will show us who He truly is and rid us of everything we thought we obtained on our own. And then we wonder why everything in our lives is falling apart and so dismantled.

At the head of this family, should seat The Creator and put nothing or anyone before Him. That's when we will come to understand why we have suffered in immeasurable ways.

He wanted to teach us a lesson. And no matter how many times God puts us through the same test, He will continue to do so until we learn whatever lesson He was trying to teach us as a whole family. Why do we blame the one's closet to us for what has transpired in our own personal lives? We forget that God gave us the family that we have for a reason. We are to be united as one yet we live our own pitiful lives as selfless and selfish individuals. We come together when it's a holiday, marriage or funeral and laugh with one another. Those are the moments we can clearly see one of the biggest elephants in the room. Why didn't you pick up the phone and say are you okay? We all needed each other at some point or another and none of us were there in a manner that was not manipulative.

Because of you family, I am in a space of ultimate spirituality where I can admit all my flaws and wrong doing opening my mind, body and soul to accept the magnificent abundance that God has for me. I apologize to all of you for whatever I have done that has not been suitable in God's eyes.

I own up to all my mistakes and not loving you the way I should have. I tried living my life to please you all and I found that to be the wrong way of living. You see, family is not about putting each other down or making fun of them, it's about holding them up and encouraging them to be the best they can. It's about unconditional love and loving them all the way God loves you. It's about helping, sacrificing, learning, intentional hugs, embracing them and caring for them the way they need at that particular moment of hardship or bliss. For those of you who thought my intentions were not of good, let me be very clear in saying, I have loved you from the moment I met you all. I have loved you unconditionally. I have loved you when times were good and bad. I can no longer blame you for the choices I have made in my life. I can only and I do mean only live for God and if that means living without you for not understanding who I am, then so be it. I have discovered my true self and it is an incredible feeling to know who I am and what my purpose is for this life on earth. I wish you all Peace, Love and God's Grace and Mercy. We will come together as a family stronger than ever if it is God's will.

I Love You All,

Tiffany Ray

"Few things help an individual more than to place responsibility upon him, and to let him know that you trust him."

-Booker T. Washington-

-Cycles of Resilience-

Ch. 15

Diary of a Homeless Woman

Dear Diary,

Empty Space.

Mattress on the floor.

Candles placed around the makeshift bed.

No furniture.

Just God and myself.

Water, soup broth and crackers were all to eat and drink.

My cleansing began.

As I sit in this quiet room I cry because God has brought me a long way. I would have been dead and gone if it were not for His grace and mercy. For every situation I thought I couldn't make it out of, He always provided a way for me The times when I thought He had forgotten about me were the hardest moments of my life. I thought God didn't love me, I thought He didn't care for me.

I substituted the love of my family isolating me with the wretched ways of the world. I've been close enough to get an understanding of what true love is but never fully knew what it would take to have that for myself. I have sacrificed everything in my life simply to be loved by others. My heart has ached every single day I have been given life.

On my quest for love, I have subjected myself to some of the most traumatic nearly homicidal and suicidal relationships. Waking up every day in fear of my life was a nightmare. Bloody noses, black eyes, busted lips, whips and lashes covering my body and bound and chained. I've been spit on, slapped, punched, drop kicked, and picked up and thrown. I was almost suffocated with a pillow; my head shoved in a toilet trying hard to breathe, held at gunpoint and forced to swallow a pistol. Sometimes I wonder how I made it out alive.

137

I've been raped countless amounts of times. It was so hard for me to look in the mirror, because I hated everything about me. I was disgusted with the thought of getting up every day to face the sadness of my existence. I was conditioned to believe that no man would ever love me. What man in his right mind would ever want me as his wife? I believed I was just another washed up and misguided fool that God had forgotten about. I hated the color of my skin, the freckles that covered my body, the color of my hair and the shape of my lips. I hated everything about my outer appearance the same way I hated my inner appearance.

I've longed to be accepted by my family but their words kept resonating in my head. Words like; I was only good for laying on my back and servicing men. I believed that I deserved to be a part of human trafficking and that sex was my niche in life. Domestic violence, rape and child abuse had been a major part of my life and its where I felt at home, because it had been consistently the same. I purposely ran away from wholesome relationships because they did not make sense to me. Instead, I embraced the worst kind of men and the unhealthiest situations because unlike everything else in my life, they had always been consistent, unchanging, unrelenting and welcoming like a cold glass of sweet and sour lemonade on a hot summer's day.

I used to believe for every time a family member said those words to me, I would be punished for that and being raped repeatedly proved that to be true to me. I blamed myself for being raped for so very long. I have been angry with everyone in my life because they never saw the good in me. I've been angry with myself and not knowing why. Depression had outweighed anything good that God was sending my way. I've spent the majority of my life crying myself to sleep begging God to save me. No matter how much good I tried to do for people it never seemed like it was enough. I have been lied on, cheated on, cursed out and put down; And for what? Because all I ever wanted was to love and be loved. I learned there was no way I was going to be able to love anyone because I didn't love myself first.

I give my heart on paper to all the people in the world who have been through or who has felt an ounce of this type of pain. It is not fair to be a human being and go through life not knowing who you are because someone inflicted their messed-up perception of themselves onto you. Forcing you to belittle yourself into thinking you are not enough. I am here to tell you and myself, we are more than enough. God was crucified, beaten and nailed to a cross where He would die. But the good news is, He died that we shall live. That is the blessing I have learned to pass along. The Creator rose again that we may live a life of peace, harmony, love, joy and service to others. He does not want such a dimmed life for us. He created us all powerful just as He. Tap into your power and you will move mountains that will instill life in not just yourself but someone who is going through the storm. Let them know that the storm will pass.

When I sit and look back over the years and how far I've come, I am certain there is a God who works miracles. You don't even know it but He's working things out for you right now. He is preparing a glorious life for you and all He wants you to do is believe and have faith that He is who He says He is. He is the Creator of all things. Every breath you take is because of Him. Even when you feel like you are drowning and there is no life vest to be found, He will pull you up and bring you out of whatever situation you feel you can't get out of. He said He will use your enemies as your footstool and I am a living testament to that. When I thought I could go no further, He grabbed hold of me and said walk with me my child. He pushed me to keep fighting, keep striving and keep thriving. No matter what anyone had to say, the Creator was with me all the way. And know that He is with you at all times. All you have to do is call His name and In a blink of an eye He will show you who He is and His wonderful works. I know that whatever situation you are faced with right now, you are not alone. There are millions of people in the world who are feeling the same way you are.

141

They are going through the same tests just like you. But you have to continue to pray your way out of it and into your predestined purposeful life.

In the process of writing this book, I was a homeless woman. No family, one friend and no one to call on. But I call on My Savior to turn things around for me and you. He put a wonderful person in my life right when I was about to give up for the last time. This person has come in and rescued me just as they were instructed by God. They came to me while I was sinking in the quick sand of life. They showed me many reasons to live. They helped me refocus in a way of tapping into my spirituality and trusting that all things will turn around for the good. They have taught me many lessons on life and understanding the dynamics of one's personality traits; why they act the way they do. Reaching down within my soul and seeing my true self for who I am and many lessons of unconditional love and kindness.

They have helped me dig deep inside of my soul and accept all that I have been through, even if it meant crying all day and night from reliving each and every situation I've faced. I had to see where I made my own critical mistakes and own up to them and not blame everyone for the way my life turned out. I forgave those that caused pain in my life and I had to forgive myself. I forgave myself so I would no longer punish me for the things I could not control or change and no longer cause self-destruction. I forgave myself that I would be able to see me. I mean really see me for the loving, caring and kind woman I am. I forgave myself so that I would be able to share all these things with you. I have let go of the past and I am looking forward to my future. I would love the same for you but you have to do the work. It's not going to be easy but it's definitely worth it. A new-found peace. Peace that you never knew existed. You cannot do it for anyone else, not your parents, children or lover. You must grow for yourself. Put YOU first and really do the work to enjoy all that God has promised you. And I know if you simply believe, apply action and know that all things will work out for the best for you, you will change lives in ways you never imagined, starting with your own. Trust me. I'm a person just like you...

To anyone who has suffered hurt, pain, agony, hatred, negativity, spitefulness, jealousy and vengeful behavior from another person, you should know that it does not matter what people think or how they feel about you and your life. It's all about what you think of yourself and what God thinks of you and how to please only Him. That is when you will find peace and solace within your soul.

Taking time to reflect on your life decisions will open a new world of ultimate possibilities. Cleansing your spirit is one of the best things you will ever do in order to heal yourself. Create daily routines and rituals for peace, clarity, understanding and freedom from the mind you are trapped in. You will see the light and overcome the hurdles of your past. Don't wait until you are on your death bed to see who you truly are. Find yourself now and learn from your mistakes.

A lot of the mistakes that I made were trusting in people to be who they proclaimed themselves to be but turned out to be the complete opposite. I was not in tune with my spirit to know the difference between someone putting up a facade or knowing who actually cared for me. I've had "friends" who portrayed themselves to be perfect but I could not see their arrogant malicious ways against me. They set plots and schemes and I fell in the trap over and over. They used what I had experienced, created rumors and attempted to sabotage a name of inner peace I was regaining. You must have a clear and leveled head to ignore the ignorance and press forward through it all.

Once you master the task of inner freedom, you will begin to explore the bountiful exquisite ways of the land your God has blessed you with. Don't hold on to grudges for if you do you are self-destructing. Love yourself and know whatever negative actions come your way, you are able to block them.

It's already been written in the stars for you. Now is the time to take your life back for you were created to love.

My writing journey has been quite enlightening to my universal self-awareness. I am capable of awakening spiritual and emotional collective consciousness to places as wondrous as the stars shining above in the atmosphere. I have transitioned into a space of self-acceptance, harmony and peace.

My journey of healing has been the ultimate testament to find who I am. With meditating, I have found that vibrations within itself healed my mind, body and spirit. Focusing on a universe beyond earth has revealed many visions. In meditation, I learned to keep my mind still while letting my inner beauty soar throughout the atmosphere to show me that I control my mind and everything that happens in my life.

The Law of Attraction states that whatever you focus your energy and attention on, whether good or bad will come to you, either wanted or unwanted. If you think about bad things, they will continue to happen. If you think of good things, that is

all that will come to you. It seems to me that we will begin to

experience levels of ultimate satisfaction when talking, thinking

and living positively. This law has changed my perspective and

outlook on life. There are many affirmations I say continuously

throughout each and every day. Affirmations for self-healing

are statements of truth which aspires to absorb into your life. I

now understand why many road blocks were set in my path. It

was a test of my faith to see if I was ready for the abundance

of blessings God has created just for me. If I never stumbled

on my journey, I would have never located the true elements of

myself. I have matured in immeasurable ways and have gained

the knowledge of God to live the way He instructs of me. In my

experience, service to others, patience, kindness, humility,

forgiveness and love are all I need to make it through each day.

Love is the most important utensil you have to create a

masterpiece of art, which you are. He is sculpting and molding

you out of the miry clay so there will only be one unique you to do His will. From the texture of your skin to the depth of your soul, God has created you perfectly.

Meditation has been my healing. When meditating, I light candles whether day or night, very light chakra vibrations to awaken the soul and sit in a place of peace with no outside sounds, distractions or interruptions. I listen for God to speak to me. I close my eyes acknowledging my breaths as I take in air slowly, deeply and at a steady pace. I clear everything from my mind and allow my true self to step forward and reclaim my life. In my daily meditations, I am free. It centers my mind and teaches it how to focus and manifest everything of joy and love into my life. Whatever I seek within my mind is given to me. I am humble for this gift and the gift of life.

For the very first time in my life, I am able to accept me for who I am. It is such a beautiful feeling to look at myself and see the beauty within, including flaws and all There is no better experience in life than to fall in love with oneself. The love I have for myself is the same love God has for me. I am willing to open my heart, mind and soul to all the endless possibilities of my heart desires. I don't desire or require much but the basic necessities of life are enough for me. Breathing God's air, feeling the wind brush across my feet or to see a child smiling is all I need. Despite it all, I'm still alive and have experienced love and met some wonderful people on my journey. God has no favorites nor does He forget about us. He is always with us to make us stronger, wiser and use us as His vessel to spread His most glorious messages. Let us live to be great and do the right things in life to help when one is in need, educate one in all avenues of life and love thy fellow neighbors, family and friends.

As I move forward with my life, I am at Peace. I am Happy. I am Humble. I am Free. I have Overcome. I am Powerful. I am Aware. I am Beautiful. I am Alive. I am a Reflection of God. I am Confident. I am Brilliant. I am Strong. I am Conscious. I am Whole. I am Educated. I am Enough. I am Awake. I know my inner self will guide me to the right decision. The more I focus my mind on the good, the happier I become. I have the power to realize my goals and obtain them. I accept my body as it is and work to make it better. Luminous and creative energy continues to flow through my veins. I am the masterpiece of my own life. I recognize and honor my talents, abilities and skills. I visualize myself having abundant wealth. My soul is pure. I have faith and deep belief in myself. I am Love. I love me. Joy overflows in my life. Possibilities are endless. Self-awareness is key. I am the person I was meant to become. I deserve to have prosperity and affluence in life. I am willing to believe I AM the creator of my own life experience. My power is in my thoughts. I am Blessed. I am Grateful. I am Thankful. I am Still Here!!! I went through the storm and stepped into better days. I have an abundance of gifts to Thank God for. And so, do YOU!!! God restored me with new life and purpose. I am no longer a victim. I am a Survivor. God gave me a voice that can no longer be silenced. Reclaim your life and begin to live in the fullness of the Creator above.

Until We Meet Again........Believe!

"You never know how or when you'll have an impact, or how important your example can be to someone else."

-Denzel Washington-